PSYCHING FOR SPORT

Mental Training for Athletes

Terry Orlick, PhD
University of Ottawa

LEISURE PRESS

Champaign, Illinois

Library of Congress Cataloging-in-Publication Data

Orlick, Terry.
  Psyching for sport.

  Bibliography: p.
  1. Sports—Psychological aspects. I. Title
GV706.4.0737 1986   796'.01   85-23293
ISBN 0-88011-273-5 (pbk.)

Developmental Editor: Linda Anne Bump
Copy Editor: Olga Murphy
Production Director: Ernie Noa
Typesetter: Yvonne Winsor
Text Layout: Janet Davenport
Cover Photography: © 1986 Dave Black
Cover Design: Jack W. Davis
Back Cover Photography: Steve Newman
Printed By: Versa Press

ISBN: 0-88011-273-5
      0-88011-275-1 (set)
Copyright © 1986 by Terry Orlick

Printed in the United States of America

10 9 8 7 6

Leisure Press
A Division of Human Kinetics
  Publishers
Box 5076, Champaign, IL 61825-5076
1-800-747-4457

Canada Office:
Human Kinetics Publishers
P.O. Box 2503, Windsor, ON N8Y
  4S2
1-800-465-7301 (in Canada only)

Europe Office:
Human Kinetics Publishers (Europe)
  Ltd.
P.O. Box IW14
Leeds LS16 6TR
England
0532-781708

Australia Office:
Human Kinetics Publishers
P.O. Box 80
Kingswood 5062
South Australia
374-0433

Other Books by Terry Orlick

Every Kid Can Win (1975) with Cal Botterill

The Cooperative Sports and Games Book (1978)

Winning Through Cooperation (1978)

In Pursuit of Excellence (1980)

The 2nd Cooperative Sports and Games Book (1982)

Mental Training for Coaches and Athletes (1982) edited with John
Partington and John Salmela

Sport in Perspective (1982) edited with John Partington and
John Salmela

New Paths to Sport Learning (1982) edited with John Salmela
and John Partington

Coaches Training Manual to Psyching for Sport (1986)

Psyched: Inner Views of Winning (1986) with John Partington

*It is not the critic who counts, not the man who points out how
the strong man stumbled, or where the doer of deeds could have done
them better. The credit belongs to the man who is actually in the
arena: whose face is marred by dust and sweat and blood; who strives
valiantly: who errs and comes short again and again; who knows
great enthusiasm, the great devotions, and spends himself in a worthy
cause; who at the best knows in the end the triumph of high achieve-
ment, and who at the worst, if he fails, at least fails while daring.*

Theodore Roosevelt

Acknowledgments

My first and most sincere acknowledgment is extended to all those athletes who worked with me on an ongoing basis, and to those who allowed me to use their names and plans in this book. They are the ones who really made it possible. I would like to thank each and every one of you—members of the Canadian canoe team, the women's alpine ski team, the women's speed skating team, and all the other individual athletes with whom I consulted over the past years.

My perspective on the applied psychology of sport was also meaningfully influenced by coaches Jack Donohue, Currie Chapman, Frank Garner, Robert Bolduc, and Lorraine Laframboise and by sport psychologists Willi Railo, Brent Rushall, Lars-Eric Unestahl, Cal Botterill, and Madeleine Hallé. Friends and colleagues who gave me valuable advice on my first draft of this manuscript included John Bales, Penny Werthner, Em Orlick, Brigitte Bittner, John Salmela, and John Partington. Linda Bump and Rainer Martens of Human Kinetics Publishers provided valued editorial assistance. Thank you all for your time and trust, and for the unique contributions you made.

C O N T E N T S

Chapter 1   **Introduction to Psyching for Sport**   1

Chapter 2   **Targets and Goals**   5

Performance Outcome Goals   6
Personal Control of Goals   8
Orientation for the Competition Day   9
Goals for the Competition Day   10
Goals   14
Training the Ideal Mental State for Competition   16
Today's Training Goals   17

Chapter 3   **Mental Plans**   19

Developing the Mental Plan   20
Self-Assessment   22

Chapter 4   **Precompetition Plan**   25

Preevent Psychological Preparation   25
Preparing Your Precompetition Plan   28
Precompetition Planning Sheets   31
Completing Your Own Precompetition Plan   31

Chapter 5   **Competition Focus Plan**   37

Event Focus   37
Extending Your Limits   39
Preparing Your Competition Focus Plan   42
Competition Focus Planning Sheets   44
Completing Your Own Competition Focus Plan   46

Chapter 6   **Precompetition Refocusing**   49
                     Lessons From Long Ago   49
                     Refocusing Before the Competition   50

Chapter 7   **Refocusing at the Event**   59
                     Refocusing Within the Competition   60
                     Refocusing After the Event   65
                     Developing Your Own Refocusing   67
                       Plan

Chapter 8   **Implementing the Plans**   71
                     Time Frame   72
                     Olympic Reflections   73

Chapter 9   **Assessing the Plan**   79
                     Postcompetition Evaluation   80
                     Filling Out Evaluation Forms   82
                     Learning From History and Unmet   83
                       Goals

Chapter 10   **Consistency and Confidence**   87
                     Enhancing Self-Confidence   87
                     Competitive Simulation   89
                     Overtraining Caution   91
                     Consistent Thoughts and Focus   92
                     Choosing Your Course   94

Chapter 11   **Building Team Harmony**   95
                     Small Group Harmony   95
                     Promoting Harmony in Training   96
                     Athletes' Suggestions for Harmony   100

Chapter 12   **Communication and Mind**   103
                     Reading
                     Mind Reading   103
                     Communication Skills   105

Chapter 13	**Relaxation and Imagery**	111
	Butterflies in Formation	111
	Relaxation	112
	Mental Imagery	114
Chapter 14	**Media Plan**	123
	Media Protocol	124
	Giving a Good Interview	127
	Guidelines for Positive Media Contact	129
Chapter 15	**Athlete's Focus—Four Case Studies**	133
	Case #1—A Winning Focus	133
	Case #2—A Relaxed Focus	142
	Case #3—A Consistent Focus	151
	Case #4—A Task Focus	158
Chapter 16	**Life After Sport**	169
	Post-Olympic Slide	169
	Making the Adjustment	175
Chapter 17	**The Last Act (or the End and the Beginning)**	177
Appendix A	**Planning Sheets**	179
	Goals	180
	Competition Reflections	181
	Personal Precompetition Plan— Content Sheet	183
	Personal Precompetition Plan— Sequence Sheet	184
	Event Focus Plan—Content Sheet	185
	Race Focus Plan—Content Sheet	186
	Game Focus Plan—Content Sheet	187
	Event Focus Plan—On-Course Format	188

Race Focus Plan—On-Course   189
    Format
Refocusing Plan   190
Competition Evaluation Form A   191
Competition Evaluation Form B   196
Mental Imagery Questions   199

Appendix B   **Precompetition Tapes and Self-**   201
                Suggestions
                Preevent Tape—Sample 1 (for rein-   202
                    forcing belief in self)
                Preevent Tape—Sample 2 (for rein-   203
                    forcing belief in collective effort)
                Additional Self-Suggestions to   203
                    Consider
                Lost Preevent Tapes   205

                References   207

Introduction to Psyching for Sport

Toady's athletes face some unique challenges. The standards are higher, the competition is tougher, the stakes are greater. Among the best, physical preparation is more complete, and the psychological component is more important than ever before. Years ago, high-performance amateur athletes may have been able to distinguish themselves in competition without developing a highly refined mental game plan, but to hope for that today is much like hoping that God will come down during a time-out to tell you how to turn a game around. It could happen, but planning on it is a little risky. As Canadian Olympic basketball coach Jack Donohue says, ''God might be at another game.''

When springboard diver Sylvie Bernier's coaches Donald Dion and Elizabeth Jack described the personal qualities that guided her to a 1984 Olympic gold medal, I immediately thought of a host of other Olympic and world champions who possess similar qualities, including

- psychological self-direction—self-disciplined, self-reliant, self-motivated;
- determination—does everything possible to reach a goal;
- organization—always sets priorities, always follows requirements to the letter; and
- concentration on task—focuses on the most relevant cues at appropriate times.

Bernier's coaches also pointed out that she performed best in, and preferred, a relaxed atmosphere or a relaxed state of mind. Sylvie had previously performed less than her best under tension and had been adversely affected by disorganization, especially when in pressure situations. She developed an effective focusing strategy for dealing with distractions, which is discussed in the next chapter. The mental qualities that she and other leading athletes have developed are critical to their performing best when it counts most.

All athletes committed to high-level performance should familiarize themselves with practical concepts and strategies for developing their mental as well as physical strength. The athlete who effectively utilizes his or her mental strength becomes stronger and more self-reliant and develops greater personal control, regardless of whether that learning is self-initiated, coach-initiated, or initiated by a sport psychologist. Coaches, teammates, sport psychologists, mental training books, or tapes may guide your growth, but ultimately mental-strength services in sport are self-directed and self-administered. *You* must select, act upon, and persistently refine a procedure for it to be most effective.

Over the past years I have worked extensively with national teams of paddlers, alpine skiers, and speed skaters and have also consulted individually with athletes and coaches from about 25 other sports including gymnastics, diving, baseball, judo, volleyball, basketball, track and field, boxing, board sailing, weight lifting, cross-country skiing, triathlon, archery, shooting, rowing, fencing, figure skating, water skiing, badminton, table tennis, and equestrian events. Athletes in each of these sports have successfully applied most of the material outlined in the pages ahead.

In writing this book I had several goals in mind. If I could sit down with you I'm sure they would be your goals too. We both want you to be the best that you can be. That means developing a psychological training program. I want to help you develop an effective precompetition plan, a competition focus plan, a refocusing plan to deal with distractions, errors, or set-backs, and a plan to improve communication. And I want you to be able to enjoy the competitive experience more, to perform consistently closer to your potential, and to acquire essential mental skills that can be utilized throughout your life.

With respect to mental training, my aim is to help you move from the thought stage to the point of action. Only if you act upon the plans we discuss will I feel I have achieved my purpose. View this as an adventure, a joint effort aimed at improving your psychological preparation. That was the spirit in which I wrote it. I invite you to read and reflect, but most of all, to act upon those reflections.

Among the athletes with whom I worked, those who ultimately became the best and most consistent performers had followed this book's basic procedures seriously and persistently. For example, they wrote down and worked on their preevent plan, event focus plan, and refocusing plan until each was highly refined. They did postcompetition evaluations in a conscientious way to draw the most from each competition and to further develop their mental strength.

When you look closely at your own best and worst performances you will discover that you can associate certain ways of feeling or thinking with your best performances. If you can plan to allow similar kinds of feelings and thoughts to surface more frequently, you will perform consistently closer to your potential.

All athletes can gain from drawing upon their own histories in order to develop their mental strength, including an effective preevent mental plan, an event focus plan, and a refocusing plan. Much of this book is designed to help you formulate those plans.

Not all the procedures or plans outlined are equally applicable to all athletes, and there are enormous differences in terms of what individual plans look like. Some athletes prefer and compete best with a very detailed, almost moment-to-moment, sequential plan. Others feel restricted by too much detail and compete best when carrying a perspective into the event, as opposed to a detailed plan. I have found that detailed plans work well for most athletes; however, I would not want you to feel that you had to develop a detailed plan or to feel guilty for not having done so.

When you read this book, do so with a certain amount of flexibility in mind. Use what you think can help you most, and adapt the material and plans to fit your personal history and present goals. Think of how the material can fit into your situation, but don't feel obligated to use something if it feels artificial or irrelevant right now. Do more than just think. Act upon your plans to improve your psychological preparation.

Targets and Goals

I n this chapter, various types of goals are discussed that relate to both training and competition. As you read through the chapter, think about specific goals you can set that will help you to really develop your physical and psychological skills. Establishing specific goals should help provide a concrete direction to your actions, give you a standard to determine whether you are attaining your goals, and encourage you to extend your limits.

Olympic basketball coach Jack Donohue tells the story of a young man who scurried up to the ticket counter at the airport, slapped $200 on the counter, and said, "Quick, give me a ticket." "Where would you like to go, sir?" asked the ticket agent. "Can't you see I'm in a hurry? I don't have time for that, just give me the ticket!" Sometimes we are in such a rush to get somewhere that we don't stop to think about where we are going or how we might best arrive.

Just as the traveler needed to define his destination in order to start on his way, athletes need to set goals to direct their efforts. Goal setting is important in sport not only because it stimulates us to think about where we can go; it also gives us a step-by-step way to get there and inspires us to take the first step. Today's goals are tomorrow's realities.

Performance Outcome Goals

First, you must decide where you want to end up. Don't sell yourself short in terms of possibilities. Dream a little. Dreams allow for the unfolding of new realities. Goals that are unimaginable are unachievable—not because they really are unachievable, but because they were never dreamt of.

With respect to overall performance goals, Norwegian sport psychologist Willi Railo points out that it is worthwhile to consider three dimensions.

First, imagine what is potentially possible if all your limits are stretched. How good could you be? *Imagine the possibility of unlimited possibility*. This should allow you to extend what you previously considered your possible upper limit. You may never achieve this "dream" goal, but if you can accept that it is within your stretched potential, then you will remove some psychological barriers that currently limit your possibilities. What you aim at affects how you approach a target, how you approach yourself, and what you are likely to hit.

Second, set a realistic performance outcome goal based on your competitive history, current skill level, and present motivation for improvement. What is the best performance you can realistically attain this year if you commit yourself to it? Think in terms of final placing, ranking, score, or personal best time.

John Bales, coach of Olympic athletes in both track and canoeing, makes a good point when he says, "A major purpose in setting a realistic outcome goal is to establish a commitment to that goal. Therefore a pretty thorough analysis should be done to make that goal a meaningful one." He suggests that a thorough analysis might be aided by sitting down with your coach and answering the following questions: (a) What is your current skill level? (b) What are your relative strengths and weaknesses? and (c) How committed are you to improving your level of performance (i.e., what is your training commitment this year compared with last year's)?

The *third* area in which you should set a goal is probably the least considered yet the most important in terms of life satisfaction: self-acceptance. Set a goal of overall self-acceptance, regardless of performance outcome. This will help you to deal constructively with unmet goals. Sometimes preestablished goals are not met even when they have been realistically set and vigorously pursued. If you fail to meet an important performance goal, you are naturally very disappointed, and there is nothing wrong with feeling and expressing that disappointment. You should still, however, be able to accept yourself as a worthy human being. I have never met an athlete who went out there and intentionally tried to perform poorly or "screw up." You should bear that in mind when responding to unmet goals. Self-damnation serves no useful purpose.

If you resolve in advance that you will accept yourself (your totality) even if a performance happens to go badly, you are less likely to suffer the kind of worry and distraction that contributes to high anxiety and poor performance. You are also less susceptible to extended bouts of depression following failure to meet goals, and consequently are freer to be human and to learn and grow as a result. In some cases, resolving to accept yourself (and those around you) regardless of the performance outcome may be difficult to do, but in the long run it is much harder not to do.

The root of almost all worry (in sport, work, and interpersonal relations) is the fear of rejection. If I fail, what will people think of me? What if I'm rejected? What if they withdraw their love, respect, admiration? Worry is rooted in your underlying assumptions about the importance of other people's evaluation of you. You can reduce that importance in your thinking with more positive, firmly grounded self-thoughts. What you say to yourself about your own value as a person affects whether or not, and how much, you worry. That is why you sometimes have to deal with your underlying assumptions (or beliefs) about yourself in relation to the situation or goal. Once you are able to *accept* yourself and your personal worth regardless of what others may think of you, or how you perform on a given day, you can keep worry in perspective.

Most often your worries about failure or rejection do not become a reality. And even if they do, the actual experience rarely brings on all the terrible things you have told yourself that they might. By experiencing an unmet goal, failure, or setback, you realize that it wasn't as bad as you thought it would be. The loss doesn't mean that you are a no-good, useless person with nothing left to live for. Life goes on. The reality is not as bad as your worrisome thoughts about it.

Personal Control of Goals

My father used to say, "If worry can solve your problems, then worry like hell." However, not many problems are solved by worrying. Worrying about what is completely beyond your control is particularly unproductive. You can't control history, judges, officials, or others' thoughts. You can, however, control yourself and your response to situations around you. In high-performance sport you should focus your energy on yourself and on the events *within your potential control.*

In a sport like alpine skiing, if you start to assume responsibility for what is beyond your control you are inviting trouble. You can't control your start number, changing course conditions, when the sun comes out, how fast or slow the snow is, when you run, how big the ruts have become by the time you ski, or your final position.

You should assume responsibilty for only that which is within your direct control: for example, how you personally ski down the hill, how well you hold your race focus, or how well you follow your race plan. You can control how well you ski down the hill in the condition you face, but you can't control the condition you face as compared with the condition others face. If for some reason totally beyond your control you are required to ski down a hill with a ball and chain attached to your leg, don't assume responsibility for the ball and chain; assume responsibility for how you ski, given the fact that this weight is attached to your leg.

If you start to get upset about something that happened, stop and ask if it was within your control. Forget about the things that only a god could control. This way you will spare yourself unnecessary anguish. If there is something you could have done to perform better in that condition, *extract the lesson* and then put the event aside.

If, after experiencing a setback or unmet goal, you go through a constructive postcompetition evaluation procedure (e.g., by filling out a competition evaluation form), it will help you to objectify the experience, learn from it, and get back on track with as little self-inflicted pain as possible (see chapter 9 for details).

Orientation for the Competition Day

Once you have dreamed a dream goal, carefully calculated a realistic performance goal, and internalized a goal of self-acceptance, the focus is always best placed upon what is immediately in front of you. Goals may project you into the future, but they must be acted upon in the present. As you approach the day of competition, you must begin to focus on components of the event within your control. Usually only a handful of athletes or teams have a realistic chance of winning any high performance contest. If all athletes go into the contest with the sole goal of winning, problems are bound to surface, because 99% of the competitors are guaranteed not to meet that goal that day. No matter how well each of those athletes performs, only one will win.

The most appropriate on-site orientation for almost all athletes to take into the competition is to give 100% of what they have. The most appropriate on-site goal for you is to maintain the event focus that you know will give you the highest probability of success. Coach Jack Donohue promotes a commitment to being "as good as I can be" as opposed to the goal of winning. The on-site commitment that he tries to instill in his players is to "play with intensity" and to "be as good as you can be," each play, each shot, each shift, this game, and this night. This kind of personal on-site goal will challenge all athletes and yet will also allow for multiple winners, based on personal best effort. Seeing how good you can be, going as fast as you can, pushing your limits, giving all you have, extending yourself, playing your game, racing your race, and doing a clean skate or routine are examples of constructive on-site orientations that often lead to best efforts, self-improvement, personal development, and sometimes winning. Frequently, however, this general positive orientation must be translated into a more specific on-site *focus*: goals that effectively and continuously direct your actions.

Goals for the Competition Day

Day-to-day goals for training and for competitions should focus on the means by which you can draw out your own potential. Daily goals should be aimed at the improvement of personal control over your performance, yourself, and the obstacles that you face. Your immediate goal is the only one over which you can ever have complete control. It is the one that will take you to your destination.

All world-class athletes have the dream of one day becoming world champion, Olympic champion, or world record holder. That underlying goal helps many athletes maintain motivation and carry intensity to training and competitions. However, when you get to the line and it is time to compete, a focus on outcome is *not* what helps most athletes perform best, even if the underlying desire is to win. You can have the goal of gold, but not while you are competing.

I have never encountered an athlete who had an all-time best performance while focusing on winning or losing *during* an event. The problem with thinking about winning or losing *within the event* is that you lose focus of what you need to *do* in order to win. In that sense it is self-defeating.

Olympic champion Larry Cain (canoeing) and World Cup champion Laurie Graham (alpine skiing) prefer to be highly energized before the start of the event and have found that thinking about wanting to win *before* the event has sometimes helped them to activate (become fired-up or charged). However, once they are at the starting line or performing within the event, the focus must give way to an effective event focus that is within their own immediate control. For Larry this meant shifting his focus to a specific race plan; for Laurie, shifting her focus to speed and the next gate.

Following his gold medal win over Olaru, the 1983 world champion from Romania, Larry Cain commented, ''I didn't look around at all during the race. I knew that if I had my best race that I'm capable of having that I could win it. I really didn't worry about what the others were doing, I just went out and followed my race plan and went as fast as I could. Things went well.''

In Kerrin Lee's first World Cup ski race, her goal going in was to place in the top 30. She was extremely nervous before the start of her race. As she approached the start she was thinking, "I know I can come in the top 30; I can improve my time by 2 seconds easily." She held onto her outcome focus *during* the run and did not ski well, placing 52nd. After that race I spoke with her about the importance of focusing on *how* to ski well rather than on outcome. Going into her next World Cup race the following day, her only goal was "to ski technically well, to ski a good clean edge, and to carry speed." Before that race she decided that she would try "to keep concentrating on what I needed to concentrate on, instead of outcome." Her thoughts as she approached the starting gate were "to ski a clean edge and to link the turns." Using this focus she was much less nervous going into the race and much more concentrated on what could get her down the hill efficiently. She broke into the top 20 (with over 120 competitors). On her race evaluation form she commented, "Today's race went really well. I was much more relaxed and I knew exactly how I had to ski to do well. I concentrated more on skiing than on outcome." When we spoke after the race, she mentioned that before the start of the race, her focus did momentarily drift to outcome. However, when it started to drift, she was able to shift back to something more appropriate before the race started. In her words, "If I did start to think that I could beat her, I would tell myself that it doesn't work that way. To beat her I have to ski right, and within 5 seconds I was back on track—back to a focus on what I had to do to ski well." She also realized in retrospect that in her best two races the previous year she had focused on skiing and not on outcome, and that in her worst races, she had done the opposite.

Many things happen on-site that will tempt you to focus on outcome: for example, reporters, TV cameras, well-wishers telling you that they've got their money on you or that you will win, as well as your own dreams and the whole competition environment surrounding you. Of course you *want* to win and *can* have a good performance outcome. But how do you do that? What focus has the best chance of allowing you to do that? Shift to that focus. You continually have to shift your focus back to where it will do you the most good.

Most athletes with whom I have worked have found that thinking about winning, or focusing on the goal of winning *before the event*, creates additional unwanted stress. They usually find that they are already activated enough, prefer to be more relaxed, or are unsure of their capacity to win. Under these circumstances, highlighting an on-site goal of winning usually increases stress or worry, takes the athlete's focus off the specific task, and is therefore not likely to be helpful.

When kayakers Alwyn Morris and Hugh Fisher came up with their all-time best performance to win the 1984 Olympic gold medal and shatter the world record by 2 seconds in the 1,000-meter pairs flat water kayak race, their only goal was to race their perfect race—to follow their own race plan, and to race as well as they possibly could. They never directly focused on winning or on other competitors *during* that race. They focused on getting from point A to point B in the most efficient, fastest way possible *for them.* Hugh never even saw his competitors during that race even though eight other boats were racing alongside him.

When an athlete's performance suffers in an important event, it is often a result of too much worry about outcome, especially in artistic and judged sports like figure skating, gymnastics, or diving, and in fine muscular control sports like archery, fencing, or pistol shooting. The winning focus is likely to heighten anxiety and interfere with proper skill execution in virtually all sports. The possibility and goal of winning may be useful for motivational purposes in training. However, once you are in the competitive situation, it is usually best to focus only on what is within your immediate control—for example, *your* serve, *your* moves, *your* pass, *your* shot, *your* execution, *your* performance. The rest will take care of itself. You can't control judges or officials and you can't control the performances of other athletes, so you can't directly control the overall outcome of the competition. You only control yourself and your performance. That is where your focus should normally be. Train hard enough to be good enough to win, then focus solely on your own performance.

Two years before the Olympics, Sylvie Bernier set her goal—to win the gold medal in springboard diving. After that point she remembers saying constantly, "Nothing will stop me! Be happy with yourself. Believe in what you are doing. Have faith in your coach. Never look back."

On a technical skill level, she knew she was capable of achieving her goal. "The most important thing for me was my mental preparation." On her road to the Olympics she set a series of intermediate goals and carefully analyzed each result. She made extensive use of mental imagery, constantly rehearsing each dive both at home and on the site. It became very easy for her to see her goals, dive by dive or in total. "I had seen myself time and time again going up to get my Olympic gold medal."

However, when Bernier won her 1984 Olympic gold medal against very powerful American and Chinese divers, she never focused on winning. She focused on doing one dive at a time, just as she had done in imagery a thousand times before. *During the competition* she never looked at the scoreboard and never asked for running scores. Between dives she listened to a cassette tape of *Flashdance*, which allowed her to stay in her own space, away from scores and away from the other divers.

One of the important lessons she had learned on the road to the Olympics was that distractions, such as looking at the scoreboard or thinking about outcomes or other divers, had resulted in her performing well under her potential. During the Olympic competition Sylvie was able to detach herself completely from the scoreboard until just before her last dive. At that point, she asked for a status report—"How am I doing, coach?" Her coach responded, "You're doing just fine." Then she nailed her last dive.

Lori Fung won the 1984 Olympic gold medal in rhythmic gymnastics by following a strategy similar to that of Sylvie Bernier. She did not watch other performers and she did not keep score. She focused only on what she had to do. Her dream goal was to win, but her on-site goal was to be consistent and to work really hard at doing each routine as best she could. After the preliminaries she was in third position, so she needed flawless routines in the finals to move into first place. She had kept track of scores during the preliminaries but for the finals she said, "I didn't want to know my scores; I just said it doesn't matter. I'm just going to go out and do four good routines and if they're good, that's great." After winning the gold medal she commented, "As each routine went, I just completely forgot about the one before. I didn't know any scores and I just said, OK, this is the only routine I have to do and I have to put absolutely every bit of energy into it; and when I finished that routine I just said the same thing for the next and the next."

There are many other examples of all-time bests occurring when athletes focus on what they have to do to perform well rather than upon where they want to finish in the standings. When Sue

Holloway and Alexandra Barré paddled their best-ever race to win the Olympic silver medal, their only goal was to follow their own race plan, to push their own limits (i.e, "follow the race plan, push the 10, go off the scale"). In a similar vein, Linda Thom won the Olympic gold in shooting by focusing her sights only on the immediate target.

In certain cases setting a goal to beat an opponent may be an asset: for example, in a team sport when going after a puck, a rebound, or a loose ball, or in a race where the best competitor is right next to you and it is the kick point in your race. The reason that setting a goal to win an encounter may *sometimes* be useful in races, team games, combative sports, and explosive events like shot putting or weight lifting is because it can inspire a greater or more complete effort, which can enhance performance. However, even in this case, to perform well you must shift back to a task focus. You can use the winning goal to energize, but you must then shift your focus to executing the task in order to perform as best you can.

Swedish sport psychologist Lars-Eric Unestahl has been a strong proponent of establishing competition-day goals that are within the athlete's control. An athlete's own performance is always within potential control; a competitor's performance is not. That is one reason a personal performance goal is often more appropriate than a goal to win. Lars-Eric points out that you should be able to visualize what you have *to do* in order to win. The *doing* should be your goal.

Visualizing winning may serve to activate you, but you should direct your actions by focusing on what you have to do to win. That is what an on-site goal should do. Of course we would all like to win. That is why many athletes and coaches invest so much of themselves. But the way to get there is to focus on the doing.

Goals

In Table 2.1 I have included Larry Cain's Goals form for the Olympic year to give you an idea of what a completed assessment looks like. Each athlete's responses are unique for that individual. Larry's dream goal and realistic goal for the year were the same, which is unusual except for athletes who are among the world leaders. You should spend some time assessing your goals using the Goals form presented in Appendix A.

Table 2.1   Goal Assessment Form for Larry Cain—Olympic Paddler

1. Dream Goal (long-term)—What is your long-term dream goal? What is potentially possible in the long term if you stretch all your limits?

   Winning always at Olympics and Worlds.

2. Dream Goal (this year)—What is your dream goal for this year? What is potentially possible if all your limits are stretched this year?

   Two gold medals in the 1984 Olympics 500 meters and 1,000 meters.

3. Realistic Performance Goal (this year)—What do you feel is a realistic performance goal that you can achieve this year (based on your present skill level, your potential for improvement, and your current motivation)?

   Same as above if best performance given.

4a. A Goal of Self-Acceptance—Can you make a commitment to accept yourself and to learn from the experience regardless of whether you achieve your ultimate performance goal this year?

   Yes.

4b. If you do not meet your desired performance goal, to what extent will you still be able to accept yourself as a worthy human being?

   Complete self-   0 1 2 3 4 5 6 7 8 9 (10)   Complete and
   rejection   full self-
                                                                       acceptance

5. Can you make a commitment to give your best *effort* (giving everything you have that day) and be satisfied with achieving that single goal?

   Yes, that's the way I approach competition.

6. Focused Psychological Goal (this year)—What do you feel is an important goal(s) for you to focus on this year in terms of your psychological preparation or mental control? For example, a *specific* goal related to psychological readiness for the event, focus control within the event, distraction control, confidence, coping with hassles or setbacks, improving interpersonal harmony or relationships?

   - *Consistency in focus control within event*
   - *Minimize distractions and loss of concentration due to less than ideal conditions*
   - *Develop ability to control myself in all race situations*

(Cont.)

Table 2.1 Cont.

---

7. Daily Goal—(a) Set a personal goal for tomorrow's training session. Write down one thing you would like to do, or accomplish, or approach with a special focus or intensity. (b) Can you set a personal goal before going to each training session this year?

    A. *Beat other racers in 250 time trials giving myself a handicap (e.g., racing pairs); in fitness testing do 150 bench presses and 45 bench pulls.*

    B. *Yes, I can set a training goal every session.*

8. What do you think you or others could do to increase the harmony among team members this Olympic year?

    Each team member can help him- or herself by learning to tolerate others better. You can not always expect others to help you, so help yourself by tolerating others.

Training the Ideal Mental State for Competition

Training should prepare you for performing in competition, not for performing in training. *What do you have to do in competitions?* Among other things you have to focus appropriately, deal with distractions, control your activation level, think positively, and extend your limits. Training goals should reflect these competitive realities. Your training should prepare you mentally and physically to meet competitive demands. The specific training goals that you establish should relate to what is needed in competition.

You will have a much better chance of doing consistently well if you have thoroughly practiced what is required in the actual competition. This means developing a precompetition plan, a competition focus plan, and a refocusing plan. It also means many time trials, competitive simulations, competitions, and careful postcompetition evaluations, so that you can become proficient at the mental and physical skills needed for excellence in competition.

If you have had a poor competitive performance, what do you do? Do you go back and work on attaining the appropriate mental state or activation level? Do you work on focus control and on the control of distractions and negative thoughts? Or do you go back and work on the wrong things? If you are a skilled athlete in good condition, and something that you can do doesn't go well in a competition, it's not very effective to go back and practice more technique or to train harder or with more intensity. You've got to work on what is likely the cause and the solution to the problem . . . your mental state *before* the event and your focus state *within* the event. By training as you wish to compete, you provide yourself with practice at these and other psychological skills.

If a performance is superb, do you spend enough time reflecting on what mental state allowed you to perform so well, and then do you attempt to make it more consistent? Do you take the time to really learn about what works for *you*? Probably the most important discovery I've made since writing *In Pursuit of Excellence* is the critical importance of understanding, refining, and directing preevent feelings and within-event focus in order to achieve *consistent* high-level performance.

Today's Training Goals

Bobby Knight, coach of the 1984 Olympic gold medalists in men's basketball, commented, "Everybody had a will to win. What we needed to talk about was the will to *practice* to win." One of the biggest obstacles to excellence is not in deciding where you want to end up, but in specifying what you are going to do *today* to get there, especially what you are going to do inside your head. Effective daily training goals ensure that today's training will help you reach tomorrow's goals. You might benefit from asking yourself the following three questions before each training session:

1. What am I going to do today (physical training/skill refinement goals)?
2. How am I going to approach what I'm going to do today (e.g., with intensity, concentration, positiveness)?
3. What am I going to do today to improve my mental strength (psychological training goals)?

Setting basic physical training goals for each workout is important. However, approaching these goals psychologically as positively as you can is equally important. To get the most out of each training session, which is what carries you to your ultimate goal, you have to go there committed to more than simply going through the motions. If you want to excel in competition, it is not enough in training just to go through the course or run through the plays or do the routine. You have to do it, or at least sections of it, with 100% intensity, with the highest quality of effort, with complete concentration.

To prepare mentally for a training session, it helps to know in advance what you are going to do and what your training goals are. Ideally, tonight you know where you are going to start and what you want to accomplish tomorrow, and you look forward to it. Then when you arrive, you are organized and ready, you know where to start, what you plan to do, and you get down to business.

It is sometimes helpful to set a personal goal or set of goals about how you are going to approach a particular workout or some segment of it. For example, for tomorrow you might decide to run with the pack or lead the pack or maintain a certain focus or positiveness for a certain portion of the workout. For each training session, decide upon one thing you would like to accomplish or approach with a particular intensity. Then do it.

I believe that setting specific training goals and bringing the highest quality of effort to training is a major factor that currently separates great athletes from good ones. In terms of pursuing your own potential, psychological preparation for training is at least as important as psychological preparation for competition.

CHAPTER 3

Mental Plans

Your head, or psych, will not miraculously improve your technical or physical conditioning. It will, however, allow you to draw the most from the conditioning you have. Today, at this very moment, your body has a certain physical capacity. If you have trained more and better, your present physical capacity will be higher than if you have trained less or less well. However, regardless of what your physical capacity might be at the moment, you have to look to your psych in order to get the most from what you have. You have to rely on your head.

All sport is psychological as well as physical because it is led by mental images and thought patterns. Your thoughts, images, and mental patterns act as the control mechanism. They direct and the body follows. The firing of a response begins in your head *before* the body responds.

Negative thought is particularly effective for destroying skilled performance. When I looked closely at the worst performances of highly skilled athletes, I found that they were almost always preceeded by negative self-suggestions. It is difficult for a body to accomplish something when the mechanism directing it (the head) says "can't," "won't," or "not able." Positive thinking or positive self-suggestion will not always help, but negative thinking almost always hurts. Controlled research using hypnosis and suggestion shows that negative suggestion to impair strength or endurance is particularly effective for weakening physical responses. It is most important to avoid or to eliminate mental directives or self-suggestions that are negative or self-defeating (e.g., "I know I won't do well," "I'll never be that good," "I'll probably blow it").

One of the major benefits of a positive psych plan is that it can hold your focus away from negative self-suggestion. In addition, thoughts, images, and mental directives that are positive, determined, and focused will often make the body respond just as you would like it to respond, and much more consistently. For example, explosive thoughts and images are particularly effective for event segments that require bursts of extreme physical exertion. You can draw from the well of your body only through fully developing your psych.

Developing the Mental Plan

Psychologically, several critical points appear to determine your performance outcome in a competitive situation. Two of these points occur in the precompetition phase, and three occur within the event itself.

Precompetition Phase

A basic precompetition plan, important for all sports, consists of an appropriate psychological warm-up combined with the physical warm-up, and an appropriate prestart focus. Through your psychological warm-up and immediate prestart focus plan, you are attempting to do three things:

1. You want to strengthen the feeling of being prepared in order to solidify your confidence in that preparation and in yourself.
2. You want to avoid the intrusion of self-defeating thoughts. They can raise the level of worry, lower confidence, or interfere with a good event, race, or game focus, thereby hindering your performance. You need to hold your attention away from worry and channel it into doing you the most good.
3. You want to help yourself enter into a more desirable preevent feeling-state, activation level, and focus to set the stage for a superior performance.

Psychological Warm-Up. First and probably most important is the general psychological warm-up that gets you into the right feeling or mental state going into the competition. It will set the stage for everything else that happens or doesn't happen. An effective pre-planned psychological warm-up combines a series of self-suggestions with well-chosen movements (and sometimes music), all aimed at creating an ideal feeling or mental state. The right pre-event feeling will increase the consistency of high-level performance.

Prestart Focus. A second crucial point is your focus of attention just before the start of the event. It should flow naturally out of a positive psychological warm-up. However, a specific prestart psych plan is also helpful. This will generally consist of a brief reminder of your event focus plan, an adjustment of your activation level, if necessary, and a focus of the first move(s) you will do, seconds before the start.

Competition Phase

The three critical psychological components of the competition itself can normally be broken down as follows:

Event Focus. How can you best focus your attention during the competition (on what, and at what points in time)?

Event Refocus. What can you do to get back on track if your focus drifts during the event? How, or on what, will you focus, or refocus, in the case of a distraction, an error, or a setback?

Through your competition focus and cues for refocusing attention within the event, you are attempting to do several things:

1. Maintain a feeling of speed, power, control, or flow throughout the event, race, or game
2. Stay on your event focus plan
3. Be able to get back on track quickly if you get off your event focus plan (or preferred focus)
4. Be sure of extending yourself to the necessary limit

Extending Limits. The third and final critical point within the event, which is not equally applicable to all sports, is your ability to mobilize all your energy and resources during the most demanding parts of the competition. Making a commitment, and having a cue to energize, to extend yourself, to push limits during critical points within the game or performance will be the final separator.

Together, the precompetition plan and the competition plan are designed to improve the consistency of your best performance, first by helping you to develop and refine an individual psych plan and then by encouraging you to implement it consistently.

Self-Assessment

The first step in developing your overall psych plan is to do a self-assessment. The most effective procedure I have found to begin this process is the use of the Competition Reflections form in Appendix A. This form allows you to reflect upon the psychological conditions of your previous best and ''not-so-best'' competitive performances. It is designed to help you draw upon your own history in competition to determine the conditions under which you have performed best. It touches on four main areas: physical activation, level of worry, self-talk before the event, and focus during the event. Because your preevent mental state and focus of attention within the event are so critical to high-level performance, it seems wise that you develop a plan, using what is likely to work best for you.

The Reflections form should make it clear how different your thinking is before a very good performance as compared with your thinking before a poor performance. It should also make evident the difference in focus within the event for a superior, as opposed to an inferior, performance. Perhaps more than anything else, your competitive reflection responses make clear the critical role that your psych plays in skilled performance. Having given these reflections forms to numerous exceptional athletes, I am convinced that in most cases the outcome of events is determined by the athlete's mental set *before* the event begins. In those cases where this does not hold true, performance outcomes are largely dependent upon the athlete's ability to properly focus or refocus attention within the event.

As you read through this Olympic athlete's reflections form, notice the clear mental differences existing between her best and worst performances, compare her activation level, her preevent self-talk and her event focus. Then complete the Competition Reflections form in Appendix A. Once you fully recognize how you focus for best results, you can begin to prepare an effective competition focus plan.

Table 3.1   Competition Reflections Responses—Skiing Sample

Knowing your racing self

1. Think of your all-time best performance(s) and respond to the following
   questions keeping that race(s) in mind:

   How did you feel just before the race?

   No activation
   (mentally and   0 1 2 3 4 5 6 7 8 9 (10)   Highly activated
   physically flat)   (mentally and
                                                           physically charged)

   Not worried   0 1 2 (3) 4 5 6 7 8 9 10   Extremely worried
   at all

2. What were you saying to yourself or thinking shortly before the start of that
   race(s)?

   Thinkin' geez, if she can do it—we can (after teammate won her first World Cup race).

   You can do it. You've had good training times; you're ready—think positive!

3. How were you focused during the race (i.e., what were you aware of or paying attention to on the way down the course)?

   *going faster . . . wanting more speed. If I made a slight error, making up the time
   . . ."look ahead, look ahead," "flow" (to where you want to be).*

4. Now think of your worst competitive performance(s) and respond to the following questions keeping that race in mind:

   No activation
   (mentally and   0 1 2 (3) 4 5 6 7 8 9 10   Highly activated
   physically flat)   (mentally and
                                                           physically charged)

   Not worried   Extremely worried
   or scared   0 1 2 3 4 5 6 7 8 (9) 10   or scared
   at all

5. What were you saying to yourself or thinking shortly before the start of that
   race?

   Usually worried about external matters that I couldn't change.

   I don't like the course conditions.

   I wonder how I'll do?

(Cont.)

Table 3.1 Cont.

---

6. How were you focused during the race (i.e., what were you aware of or paying attention to on the way down the course)?

   Little things were bugging me.

   I was worring too much rather than becoming aggressive.

7. What were the major differences between your thinking (or feelings) prior to these two races (i.e., best and worst)?

   In the good performance I believed in myself and felt confident. In the poor performance I lacked the "spark" to want a good result. I didn't think I could do it.

8. What was the major difference in your focus of attention during these performances (i.e., best and not-so-best)?

   In the poor performance my attention was focused on external problems (snow, race organization, etc.). In the good performance it was on me—on what I could do.

9. How would you prefer to feel just before an important race?

No activation (mentally and physically flat)	0 1 2 3 4 5 6 7 8 ⑨ 10	Highly activated (mentally and physically charged)
Not worried or scared at all	0 1 2 ③ 4 5 6 7 8 9 10	Extremely worried or scared

10. How would you prefer to focus your attention *during* an important race?

    I would rather have my attention focused closer to me—on things that concern myself only—not letting the outside come into my shell . . .

11. Is there anything you would like to change about the way you approach a race? Or training?

    To have consistent thoughts and focuses going into the races to make my results consistent.

12. Is there anything you would prefer to change about the way the coach approaches you during training or competitions?

    I would like positive comments from the coaches during races without any relating to anything negative.

Precompetition Plan

I f we look at high-performance athletes' previous best performances, the following commonalities surface:

- They trained hard and well.
- They generally entered the event with their own thoughts, feelings, and beliefs on their side (i.e., constructive self-talk, positive feelings, belief in capacity).
- Before and during the event, they were free from negative or self-defeating thoughts and were not distracted by high levels of worry. That, in turn, appeared to free their bodies and focus for a peak performance.
- They were highly activated before the event but were *not* feeling extremely anxious or overcome by worry.

Part of your objective in preparing an effective precompetition plan is to create these and other conditions that will allow for your best performances to occur more consistently.

Preevent Psychological Preparation

A constructive psychological warm-up normally consists of realistic, positive self-suggestions, imagery, and a well-established pattern for combining these skills, which make even the most stressful competitions seem more normal.

Realistic Self-Suggestions

Preevent positive thinking should be grounded in reality, based on real strengths, and specific in content (e.g., base it on how well you have prepared, on your capacity to push yourself, on the fact that you have performed extremely well on certain previous occasions, and on your capacity to perform at least that well again). Self-talk leading to unwanted increases in preevent worry should be altered, eliminated, or replaced with a more appropriate focus. Self-suggestions or reminders about such things as preparation, readiness, ability, adaptability, or commitment to give everything you have are normally included in the psychological warm-up.

Imagery

There will likely be great diversity in terms of the specific content of different athletes' preevent plans. Some of you will feel most comfortable with activating thoughts, some with calming thoughts, some with very organized, detailed reminders, and others with less organization. For some athletes, listening to a certain song or recalling a certain image or perspective is all that is needed to create their preferred preevent state. Most athletes find that a reminder of their preferred on-site event focus is useful just before the start of the event. The closer you get to the event, the more important it is to focus specifically on the task that lies directly before you. This focus has to be flexibly applied to meet your individual needs.

A mental review or imagery of the game plan (or parts of the game plan) is also usually included in a constructive on-site psychological warm-up. Some of the thoughts or images may occur while you are physically active during your warm-up or during short breaks from movement. Generally, the most extensive use of imagery or reminders about how you plan to focus during the event occurs when you are in your "own space" with your own thoughts during the final moments of psychological preparation before the event. For example, when sitting or lying quietly or when walking away from the crowd, you may choose to call upon reminders of good training, use imagery of past personal bests, mentally review your event focus, or recommit to extend 100%. Immediately before performing, often the most important thing to draw out of your imagery is the "feeling" of a good performance, the "feeling" of executing the first few moves perfectly, or the focus associated with that feeling (see the Imagery section in chapter 13 for additional suggestions). Positive self-suggestions and reminders such as those listed below can be useful during your general warm-up or during your final prestart preparations. (See Appendix B for additional suggestions.)

- I have *prepared* extremely well, both physically and psychologically.
- I am *capable* of adapting to any environmental condition. The wind, the lane, the course, the competitors make no difference. I am *in control* (of me).
- My goal is realistic and *I can achieve it*. Nothing will disturb me; nothing will distract me.
- Draw from the well. *Extend* yourself. Stretch your limits.
- Follow your *plan* and you will be flowing in control throughout.
- I am *ready*; I am my *best*. Do it!

These precompetition suggestions assume that you have prepared well for this event. They may even serve as a basic guide for your overall training because they remind you of how you want to feel as you go into this competition. You want to train so that you can say these things at the competition site and believe them.

Your immediate prestart thoughts, the ones you use as you approach the starting blocks, can focus on the task (e.g., "race my race"), on a final positive thought (e.g., "I *am* totally prepared, I know I can do it"), or on your final activation level, (e.g., breathing out slowly, saying "relax," or pumping up a little, saying, "This is it—*do it*").

The following statements are examples of self-suggestions and reminders used by high-performance racers *immediately before* their best performances (e.g., just before they left the starting block).

Final Task Focus.

- Race my race.
- Think about what I am doing, not about what anyone else is doing.
- Start fast, hold on, concentrate.
- Go with them (leaders), stay with them, then kick.
- Concentrate.

Final Positive Thought.

- I am totally prepared—I know I can do it.
- Go out and do what you are capable of doing.
- I will perform better than ever before.
- I have prepared properly—the work is done.
- I am the best—I am my best.
- I can do it. Just go out and do it.

Final Activation Control.

UP (to boost activation)
- Really go for it—no matter how much it hurts.
- This is it; I have to do it, now.
- Go until I die.

DOWN (to lower activation)
- Breathe, relax, calm down.
- Relax; you know you will do well.
- It's only training.
- Calm, in control.

One of the equestrians with whom I worked gave me some interesting feedback regarding the use of precompetition self-suggestions. After thinking about her preevent plan, she decided to include phrases like "I am strong," "I am ready," "I am good," "I am the best." But when it came time to actually say these things before the event, she recalled that "I thought I didn't really need it. I thought to myself, I already know that. I felt stupid about doing it and almost didn't. But then I said, 'What the heck, I'll try it.' And as I started to repeat those phrases, my body reacted. My body language changed completely; I stood taller and walked with more assurance. It was as if my head knew these things but my body didn't until I started repeating some of these thoughts. I felt great and rode great."

Preparing Your Precompetition Plan

When first attempting to develop a preevent plan and event focus plan, look closely at your responses on the Competition Reflections form in Appendix A. Some athletes have also found it helpful to review their diaries or logs from the previous season. If you can recall how you focused for previous best performances, often specific phrases, cues, and focus points can be drawn out and tied into your mental plan. Start by writing down a plan based on the kind of psychological warm-up and prestart focus that has already worked for you. This will give you a base, which you can gradually refine. Writing things down makes you think about how you really want to feel and focus. It also helps clarify what you can do to help yourself feel that way. If you never stop long enough to understand exactly what you are doing mentally, or if you do something different every time, it is difficult to know what and how to refine. Writing down your plan(s) gives you something specific to apply, evaluate, and refine. The overall process helps you understand how to act on your strength more often and more consistently.

When attempting to refine your preevent plan during the season, draw from your Completed Competition Evaluation forms (see chapter 9 and Appendix A). Over the course of a season your perspectives may change, and personal growth will occur. Therefore, alterations in plans for personal bests may be required.

When you first devise your preevent plan, it is most critical that you draw upon the thoughts and procedures that served you best in the past. If you compete in a sport with multiple events (e.g., figure skating, skiing, a 3-day equestrian event, or gymnastics), you will know that different events often have different requirements. For example, performing compulsory figures requires a much lower activation level than performing the short free-skating program. Similarly, a relaxed, calm composure is most likely to keep a gymnast on the balance beam, whereas a very high activation level is likely to help her explode off the take-off board into a vault over the horse. Be sure to develop a plan to meet your personal requirements for each of your events and to write it out on the Precompetition Planning sheets provided in Appendix A. Some athletes prefer to have two precompetition plans, one for a day when things are going well and another for a day when things are not going so well. The following suggestions were given to a member of the National Ski Team who preferred this two-plan approach. The suggestions were drawn from her personal history of best and worst races.

Plan A: Normal Procedure

Psychological Warm-Up. Make sure you warm up well (e.g., good stretching and plenty of warm-up runs). Know the course well, study it thoroughly, and use imagery. In your imagery before the downhill run, "feel the course on the way down; feel it in sections—be aggressive." Before the GS (Giant Slalom) feel the course in terms of "rhythm" and "finesse" rather than driving. Go through the course in your mind *feeling* the way you like to feel.

In the final minutes at the top, stretch; use imagery of the course while moving your body with the imagery. Before you get into the starting gate make sure that your heart rate is up and that you are physically activated. Do active movement beforehand—jump up and down, jump side to side, do tucks; get physically and mentally ready to blast out of there—with *intensity*. Feel yourself becoming *energized* before the start. Remind yourself, "You can do it. You're ready."

Prestart Focus. Seconds before the start, breathe in—breathe out (relax on exhalation); get the image again of your ideal skiing feeling (energized skiing). Give yourself a final reminder of your best race focus (speed); begin narrowing focus, seeing only the course; *Explode* out of the gate. *Go! Push It!* Focus ahead *gate, gate, gate.*

Plan B: Not-So-Great Day

Let's say you have had a couple of relatively poor training days or training runs and are beginning to feel less inspired.

Psychological Warm-Up. Remind yourself that you still have the ability to race well today. You have had days with underwhelming training runs and still had a good race. You don't lose your ability to ski from one day to the next. You may, however, lose your concentration. To turn it around, commit yourself to a good race. Search for speed and let it go. Remind yourself of your capacity; remind yourself that you have turned it around before. Increase your use of imagery; for example, visualize yourself skiing the way *you* can ski and feeling the way you want to feel.

Prestart Focus. Then focus fully on following and feeling your prerace plan as outlined in Plan A. Enjoy it!

Precompetition Planning Sheets

The following Precompetition Planning sheets will give you some idea of how to develop your own plan. Table 4.1 is the general guide that was given to athletes to help them develop their own plans. This form is divided into four basic categories of precompetition activities: general physical warm-up, general psychological warm-up, start preparation—physical, and start preparation—psychological. To demonstrate how an Olympic athlete transferred this general guide into a personal precompetition plan, Dee Dee Haight, an alpine skier, agreed to share her plan. In Table 4.2, Dee Dee outlined the content of her plan as she wanted it to occur under each of the four categories. In Table 4.3 she drew upon the information generated from Table 4.2 and outlined her precompetition plan in the sequence in which she wanted it to occur at the competition site. She then worked on implementing that plan (see chapter 8, ''Implementing the Plan'').

The final precompetition form presented in this chapter is drawn from the sport of flat water paddling. Table 4.4 outlines the on-water, preevent sequence plan used by Sue Holloway, Olympic silver medalist. Although it is different from Dee Dee Haight's plan, it was effective for Sue. Preevent plans must be prepared to meet individual needs.

Completing Your Own Precompetition Plan

When you complete your own precompetition planning sheets, include the *specific* mental and physical activities you plan to do under each category (e.g., how many starts you will do, what self-suggestions or reminders you will include). Then outline your entire precompetition plan in sequence just as you would like it to unfold at the competition site. Draw upon what has already worked for you in the past for your best performances and upon what you feel should work best for you. Use the Precompetition Planning sheets in Appendix A.

Table 4.1 General Guide for the Precompetition Plan—Content

General Physical Warm-Up	General Psychological Warm-Up	Start Preparation—Physical	Start Preparation—Psychological
• Easy stretch and run • Free skill practice • Simulate important segments of competition	Establish comfort zone with competition area (inspection, own space, imagery), reminders of potential and strengths, positive imagery, reassuring self-statements, reminder of on-site goals to establish the best focus and perspective	Specific preplanned individual and/or team warm-up	Specific preplanned preevent thoughts: brief mental review, adjust activation level *if necessary* (breathe-exhale-relax), reminder of complete readiness (just do it); once in ready position, focus on task immediately in front of you

Table 4.2 Personal Prerace Plan—Content for Dee Dee Haight (Alpine Skiing)

General Physical Warm-Up	General Psychological Warm-Up	Start Preparation—Physical (at the top)	Start Preparation—Psychological (at the top)
• Wake up feeling good; optimistic but not unrealistic	• Think positively of myself; not think of who or what I have to perform for	• Begin light stretching, increasing to intense physical activity as start time closes in	• Funnel approach to start preparation—from happy and confident to centered and focused
• Morning run; stretch	• Mental calm and relaxation		
• Free skiing—aggressive and pumped, yet calm and relaxed	• Thoughts of what makes me happy "away" from skiing while riding lift or sitting in lodge		• Begin by thinking of things that make me happy, mentally at ease, relaxed, and confident
• Enjoy the skiing	• Concentrated or focused while skiing		• As the start time closes in, center on what I've got to do to perform
			• Reminders that I can do it, avoiding negative thoughts or intrusions

Table 4.3 Personal Prerace Plan—Sequence for Dee Dee Haight (Alpine Skiing)

General Warm-Up Physical and Mental	Start Preparation Physical and Mental

Night Before Race:

- Receive number, determine how many minutes after start I run (race)
- Figure out what time to awaken and leave for hill in the morning, and approximately how many free runs or training course runs to have before start
- Estimate how long to put number on, stretch inside lodge
- Spend ideally no more than 20 to 25 min in start area

Morning of Race:

- Light run, exercises, begin the morning on a positive or high note
- Wake up feeling good about myself, be optimistic, flow
- Important for me not to project (e.g., about outcomes); just feel good about myself for myself
- Free skiing and training courses to feel aggressive and pumped, yet calm and relaxed
- Focused and concentrated while skiing
- Mental imagery (to know course and feel good about myself on course)

- Arrive at start 20 min prior to my start
- First get race skis in snow, check them to see if all is ready; see rep. (equipment person)
- Begin stretching, running; think happy, relaxed thoughts; mental imagery of the course
- Listen to coach's comments (being relayed up the hill)
- Apply these comments to mental imagery
- Heavier physical preparation
- Get into skis, binding check
- More imagery of race focus and feeling—include correction imagery if needed
- Quicker physical activity
- 1 min—take coat, warm-ups off, intense, focused on task
- 30 sec—ready myself in start; think only of course and of getting to the bottom
- Explosive start

Table 4.4 Personal Prerace Plan—Sequence for Sue Holloway (Paddling)

2,000-Meter Warm-Up

- Stay loose
- Just another time control
- Going to give it everything

If a little flat remember,

- Takes a while to warm up
- I'm ready, I'll be able to do it

500 Meters at 70%

- Reach out
- Keep it long
- Put an effort into it, concentrate

250 Meters at 90%

- Need to work hard and I will be fast

3 × 20 Strokes at 100%

- 3 starts

Prestart

- Deep breaths—relax shoulders and grip
- Follow the race plan and give 100%
- Look ahead 15 ft
- Mentally rehearse first strong strokes

If Distracted

- Look only down my lane
- Concentrate on first strokes
- Take deep breaths to relax

Competition Focus Plan

I f we look at top athletes' best performances, it is clear that their focus allowed
them to remain completely "connected"
to the task before them. The purpose of
this chapter is to help you develop a specific competition focus plan
to carry you over the distance of the race, game, or event in the
best possible way.

Event Focus

The best focus will depend upon your individual makeup and
the demands of your particular sport or event. Many sports can
be broken down into critical parts or sequential checkpoints. For
example, a short-duration (2 to 4 min) sport like flat water canoe
racing can be divided into sequential focus points. The first critical
focus point would be the start of the race, that is, focusing on a
certain number of deep powerful strokes, followed by a specific
number of lighter strokes to reach race pace. The remainder of the
race would consist of following a basic race plan with pace checks
and pick-up points at several preplanned points such as at 1/5, 2/5,
3/5, and 4/5 points in the race. At these preplanned points on the
course, the paddler can check to ensure that the pace or stroke rate
is on, and adjust it if it is off. The body can also be scanned peri-
odically to remove unwanted muscular tension or to focus on
"form," "smooth," "reach," "pace," or "pick-up," depending

upon the point in the race. Preplanned checkpoints and focus cues are designed to help the athlete perform efficiently and to stay on the event plan.

Team games like ice hockey or basketball cannot normally be broken down into sequential checkpoints. However, they can be broken down into critical parts or critical situations, which do not necessarily occur in any particular sequence. For example, in hockey, critical situations might include the first 2-minute shift, a goal against, a goal for, a loose puck in the corner, a missed shot, offense in the slot area, a penalty, or the beginning and end of the final period. In each of these critical situations the athlete should know what he or she wants to do and should have an effective focusing plan to do it.

In the 1984 Winter Olympics, a young Canadian hockey team held a powerful USSR squad scoreless for the first period-and-a-half of play. Then the Soviets scored, and within 2 minutes they scored again. Did you ever see sharks after they make their first strike? Something "juices" them to the point that nothing could possibly deter them from getting to their target. That is the image that surfaces when I see the best Soviet hockey players respond to a scored goal. Their movements remain controlled and determined, but they are going after that target—pass, pass, pass, pass, score. The consistency and swiftness with which second goals are scored after the first strike makes me feel that it is a preplanned pick-up point. If it isn't, it should be, because this is a critical point in the game for both teams.

A preplanned commitment and cue to pick up the pace and go all out for the few minutes immediately following any score are important. They are especially important for a team that has been scored against because the scoring team gets a natural lift from its score. In the example cited above, if the Canadian team had prepared themselves to quickly put aside their disappointment resulting from the first goal scored, and had immediately focused on picking up their own pace, perhaps that second strike would not have occurred, or at least not so quickly.

Having a team strategy for collectively focusing or energizing in the face of adversity can be effective. For example, after a goal against, each player might benefit from a personalized cue that signified "attack," "go," "push it." One person will have a tough time turning things around himself, but a collectively timed and focused "pull" can do wonders for the team and for the struggling individual.

In events that continue over long periods of time, such as marathons or triathlons, as well as in some dual sports and team sports, it seems best to have some general psychological cues and also to break the event down into critical parts. General cues serve as reminders that you can use throughout the event or game whenever needed to maintain your best focus. They may be related to technique ("stay low," "stretch," "pull"), to a relaxed focus ("relax," "flow," "smooth," "easy"), or to self-encouragement ("I can do this," "I want this"). If, in addition to developing these general cues, you can break your event into critical situations and prepare specific cues for dealing with each of these situations, you will have a good chance of holding your best focus throughout the event.

A triathlete using this approach found that general reminders of a relaxed inward focus, mostly on her own body awareness and on thoughts of "fast," "relaxed," and "in control" worked best in most situations. To break her race into critical parts, she used the following specific preplanned focus points:

1. *At the start*. Establish "position," then think, "Long, powerful, loose stride, rhythm."
2. *Early in race*. As field starts to thin out, think, "Maintain pace, form, tuck in behind someone, loosen up."
3. *Middle of race*. Think, "Keep going, don't let up, feeling good, relax, flow."
4. *Later in race*. At an extending point, think, "Pain is mental, push beyond the pain, pace, inward focus."
5. *End of race*. Think, "Finish it off, push it in, power, strong, go for it, drive."

Extending Your Limits

Very little separates athletes at the highest level; consequently, it is extremely important for you to psychologically prepare to push limits toward the end of your event, for example, during the last 1/5 of the distance or at a critical point in a game. This can make the difference between accepting your effort or feeling that you gave up, between being in the medals and out of the medals, between 1st and 4th, between 3rd and 8th, and easily between world champion and *almost* world champion. At this level, all athletes' muscles burn with fatigue toward the end of a demanding event. Some will push beyond it, some won't. That will make the difference.

When normal, untrained people are confronted by fatigue signals, they do the sane thing: They slow down or stop and thereby protect their untrained, sometimes fragile bodies. When you are faced with fatigue signals, you may also be tempted to slow down because it seems like the easiest and sanest thing to do. Your muscles are tired and you hurt, so you ease up, stop, take a rest, and have a cold drink.

However, if you listen to fatigue signals and interpret them in the same way as untrained people, you will fall short of your goals and potential almost all of the time. You can't achieve high-level goals by acting like a normal, untrained person. You have to move beyond sanity to a higher level. Some people call it insanity—high-level insanity. (That's a joke in case you aren't smiling.)

For trained athletes, muscles screaming with fatigue do not normally represent a physical risk, nor are they a valid indication that there is nothing left in the muscle. It's a question of calling upon the reserve that remains. It is a cue to begin drawing from the well. Committing yourself to do this *before* the race or game begins will help immensely as will highly energized cue words in response to a predetermined kick point(s) (e.g., a certain point on the course). Fatigue can also be used as a signal to pickup. Muscles or bodies that are burning with fatigue toward the end of a race or at a critical point in a game can be used to trigger helpful responses. For example, preplanned and prepracticed cue words that carry emotion, thought flashes, or focus points can help with the final critical push.

For energizing cues to be effective under fatigued conditions, they must be stated or thought *forcefully with emotion* and conviction in order to override the emotion associated with the feeling and negative self-talk that accompany fatigue. Many athletes have used the following cues effectively:

Cue words:
- GO, GO
- PUSH

- EXTEND
- DO IT, DO IT, GO FOR IT
- POWER, POWER
- I CAN, I CAN.

Thoughts:
- Don't give up an inch.
- You've trained too hard to let it slip away.
- Refuse to let him or her pass you; refuse to let him or her get the puck/ball.
- There's no tomorrow.
- It will be all over in another 10 seconds (1 minute, etc.).

Focus points:
- Count strokes, strides.
- Focus on the finish line.
- Focus on the object or person in front of you—go for it.

Some athletes (mostly males) have reported that the use of swear words generates a much higher charge than a simple cue word such as "go" or "push." In some cases the emotion-filled swear word is directed at the nearest competitor: For example, "I won't let you PASS, you _____ ." In other cases it is directed at the self: "GO, GO you _____ ! How many times in your life will you have this chance?" I'm not advocating this approach but simply pointing out that for some athletes it works.

Developing a competition strategy to push or stretch to your capacity is critical. If you want to perform to your limit, you have to train to push so that your psych can fire that energized response you want and so that your body (motor units) becomes trained at performing skillfully under the most demanding conditions.

In training to push your limits, two points should be considered. First, you cannot train at a high level of intensity all the time. That can result in overtraining and diminishing returns. So it is important to select certain days for high-intensity simulation training and to plan those days in advance. You are choosing to work at such a high intensity for those specific days, primarily because developing the ability to really push yourself and to focus properly while doing so, especially when fatigued, makes all the difference in a competition.

You can set personal goals for extending yourself on those selected training days. You can also begin to ask yourself, Did you draw from the well? Did you completely extend yourself? That is a good question to ask after training and after competition. Often it is a *better* question to ask *before* the event, when you can still do something about it. Will you draw from the well?

In a single year some high-performance athletes will train over 1,000 hours to race for 2 or 3 minutes. It always struck me as strange that athletes could train so long and so hard and then not draw from the well, not fully extend themselves, during that final 2-minute test or during the final seconds of that challenge.

It won't kill you to draw fully from the well. It won't kill you to push to your limits within your event. It will hurt, it will burn, your muscles will scream, you will be completely exhausted temporarily, but it won't kill you. So why come across the line, or finish the game, knowing you could have or should have done more? At the time you may have thought that the well had run dry, but if you had reached down a little further, you likely would find another cup of water, another cup of energy.

When highly conditioned athletes fail to draw from the well, it is usually a result of their not making a preevent commitment to do so or not having a focus strategy to do it within the event. It is closely tied in to a personal commitment to go after personal goals. Once the preevent commitment has been made and the mental strategies are in place, the limits are extended.

Preparing Your Competition Focus Plan

When attempting to develop an effective competition focus plan, closely review what has already worked for you for your previous best performance. Your goal is to devise a plan that will allow you to focus all your energy and resources into doing you the most good. The focus that will do you the most good will depend upon your personal characteristics, your history, and your sport.

In the sport of alpine skiing, the hill provides the speed and momentum; the skier reads and reacts. Generally the best focus (the fastest and most flowing) in the race is down the hill, slightly ahead of yourself, to where you are going: "Look ahead, look ahead; gate, gate, gate, search for speed; let it go." If you have studied the course well and are focused ahead, you should be able to automatically and continually adjust to what lies ahead and do as little as possible to get around the gate. Competition is not the time for technical instruction; it is the time to trust your body, to focus ahead, and to go. When you have reached a high skill level and have skied down many hills many times, your body and mind know how to get down a hill quickly. You simply have to free yourself to do it.

In sports centering around reading and reacting, which also include many dual and team sports, a technical focus during the competition is not likely to be helpful. The problem with a technical focus is that if you are focused on and conscious of some technical or mechanical point under you or in your body, you cannot also be focused ahead ("reading" what is coming) and going after the hill, ball, or puck ("reacting") with the needed intensity. This is not to say that you never have to work on technique. However, if technical correction is needed, the conscious attention to improving technique should ideally occur in training and be automatic by the time you get into the competition.

In the sport of speed skating, unlike alpine skiing, the athlete generates his or her own speed and momentum and races in a relatively controlled situation where there is not much need to read and to react. To generate and maintain speed, the skater must bend at the waist and maintain a very streamlined body position. Good skating technique—staying low, pushing the skate to the side, and pushing harder on the outside skate on the corners—is critical to efficiency of movement. If a skater loses his or her technique or body position even momentarily, that transfers directly and dramatically into a loss of self-generated speed. Generally, the best focus (fastest and most flowing) in this type of race is on skating technically well. This often necessitates reminders to "stay low," "push to the side," "relax," "lean," "push hard," "race your race."

If you look at your own sport and your own performance history in your sport, you will discover what sort of focus works best for you. Do you perform better when you focus on just "going" and letting your body automatically plug in technique, or do you end up "spinning your wheels" when you do this? Do you perform better when you focus on maintaining the proper technique, or does some combination of technical reminders and "letting it go" work best? That is something you will discover by developing your focus plan and by experimenting with it.

Competition Focus Planning Sheets

The following Competition Focus Planning sheets will give you some idea of how to develop your own plan. Table 5.1 and Figure 5.1 outline the race focus plan used by Olympic skier Dee Dee Haight. On Table 5.1 Dee Dee breaks her race focus into four parts: the start, first few gates, course, and finish. On Figure 5.2 she transferred the content of her basic race focus plan to an on-course format.

Table 5.1 Race Focus Plan—Content for Dee Dee Haight (Alpine Skiing)

Start	First Few Gates	Course	Finish-Last Few Gates
• Really "*explode*" and "*push*" • "Flow" in the first crucial part of the course • Get into it! • "Feel good" from the start • Be "precise"	• "*Speed*," "aerodynamic," "riding a flat ski" • Focus on the "*gates*" or section "here" and "now" • Take calculated risks, "get to the bottom," but be aware of what must be done	• Focus only on what must be done in order to finish quickly • "Center" on getting to the bottom but aware of what I'm doing *now* • A controlled but uncontrolled level of skiing—"*let it go*"	• Continued concentration • Be mentally strong • "Squeeze" the few extra tenths, hundredths • "*Push*" • "Work" the last gates" • It isn't over till I stop in the finish area

Start Area	First few gates	Course	Last few gates finish

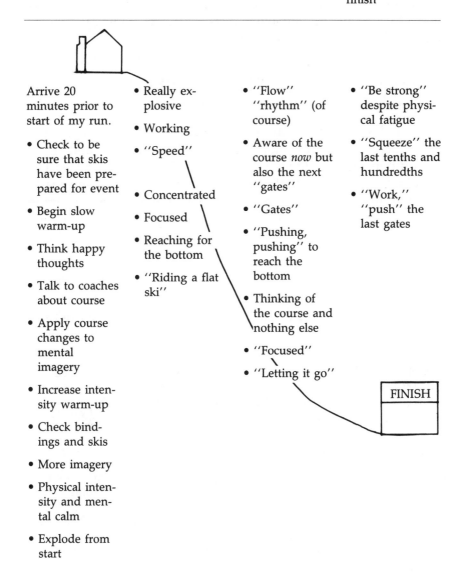

Arrive 20 minutes prior to start of my run.

- Check to be sure that skis have been prepared for event

- Begin slow warm-up

- Think happy thoughts

- Talk to coaches about course

- Apply course changes to mental imagery

- Increase intensity warm-up

- Check bindings and skis

- More imagery

- Physical intensity and mental calm

- Explode from start

- Really explosive

- Working

- "Speed"

- Concentrated

- Focused

- Reaching for the bottom

- "Riding a flat ski"

- "Flow" "rhythm" (of course)

- Aware of the course *now* but also the next "gates"

- "Gates"

- "Pushing, pushing" to reach the bottom

- Thinking of the course and nothing else

- "Focused"

- "Letting it go"

- "Be strong" despite physical fatigue

- "Squeeze" the last tenths and hundredths

- "Work," "push" the last gates

FINISH

Figure 5.1 Race Focus Plan—On-Course Format for Dee Dee Haight (Alpine Skiing)

The race focus plan for Larry Cain, 1984 Olympic champion in flat water canoe racing, is outlined on Table 5.2 and Figure 5.2. On Table 5.2, Larry outlined his preferred, or best focus for various stages of the 1,000 meter race. On Figure 5.2 he outlined the same basic plan, but in this case transferred it onto an on-course format that attempted to give a better feel for actually paddling down a lane on the race course.

Completing Your Own Competition Focus Plan

Decide how you want to feel, focus, and function during the various phases of your event. Then devise a focus plan for that to happen. Look closely at your Competition Reflections form. Draw upon the cues and focus points that have already helped you perform best in your past. When reading through the focus plans of other high-performance athletes in the remainder of this book, attempt to draw out perspective or focus cues that might be applicable or adaptable for your situation. Try to implement your focus plan, and then refine it with the help of the Competition Evaluation forms in Appendix A.

If you have confidence in your coach, it is helpful to sit down with him or her to discuss your focus plan. Your coach may be able to help break your event into meaningful segments and may also suggest appropriate focus points (or cues) for various segments.

If you are involved in a team sport, your coach may be able to help you list critical situations you are likely to face within a game and to indicate how he would prefer for you to respond in each of these situations during the game. You can then think about what you feel would be your ideal on-court response to each of those situations. In devising your focus plan, draw upon the focus that has worked best for your previous performances in that situation. Also draw upon what you feel will work best for you. Think of cues or reminders that will allow you to hold your preferred focus and bring on your preferred response. Then practice them. Use the Competition Focus Planning sheets in Appendix A to write out your plan.

Table 5.2 Race Focus Plan—Content for Larry Cain (Canoeing)

First 5th		Second 5th	Third 5th	Fourth 5th	Final 5th		
Start	Transition					Kick Point	Final Push for Finish
3 deep power strokes	3-4 sprint strokes—extension to full extension in 3 or 4 strokes	*Pace, form, flow, relax* (checking constantly) Focus down lane Power only, not rate	*Catch, power in the water* Power burst at ½ way (½ way surge) keep momentum	*Technique*	Preexplosion Breathing, strong exhalation	Explode New race All or nothing Narrow focus to only finish line and power Deep crisp strokes	Shoot boat

Outline your race plan as you would like it to occur. Include your cues and focus points at various stages in the race.

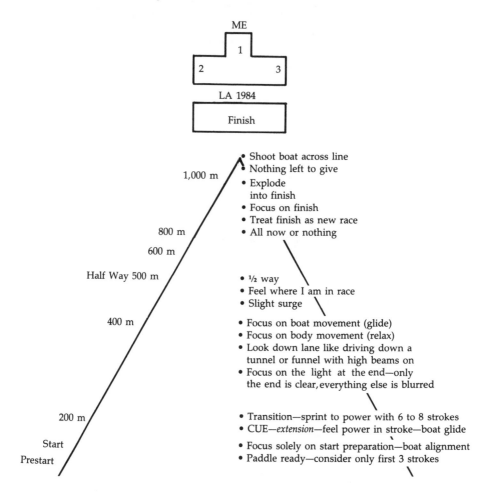

Figure 5.2 Race Focus Plan—On-Course Format for Larry Cain (Canoeing)

Precompetition Refocusing

What happens to you is nowhere near as important as how you react to what happens to you.

Jack Donohue

Refocusing appropriately before, during and after the competition is one of the least practiced but most important skills for high-performance athletes. A refocusing plan is aimed at helping you to refocus away from unwanted external distractions or internal distractions such as worries, self-doubt, and self-put-downs.

Lessons From Long Ago

I have learned some important lessons about refocusing by studying the games and lifestyles of aboriginal people. Several years ago, I spent 6 weeks living in a remote village in the jungles of Papua New Guinea. I was impressed with a traditional ritual for ending competitive games that had passed down through the ages. At the end of the game, the group came together, and as one player touched every other player, he or she said, "I take it from you." He or she then walked over to a tree and placed his or her hand on the tree. Taking "it" from everyone and putting "it" into the tree was done to ensure that no one left the game with bad feelings. When playing in the water, teams sometimes chanted together "1, 2, 3," and all slapped "it" into the water or threw "it" to a nearby tree. The anxiety or animosity that may have lingered within players was thereby laid to rest.

This ritual grew out of the wisdom of ancestors who recognized that bad feelings could sometimes surface in competitive games. Going through the motions of physically removing anger, anxiety, or bad feelings increased the chances of leaving those feelings behind.

The same concept can be effectively applied in the modern world of sport—for training, for precompetition hassles, for distractions within the competition, or for postgame blues. Let's say that on the way into your training session or class you are bothered about an argument that occurred at home. You know that it will not help you, or the situation, to think about it during training. You want to set it aside—"tree it" for the next 2 hours. So as you enter the gym or class, you press your hand against the wall or door and think, "tree it." At that point you smile and say to yourself, "I am going to be here for 2 hours and I am going to get the most out of being here. Upon leaving, you may want to consider how you will deal with the argument. Or if you want to feel miserable again, you can replace your hand on the wall to recapture that "treed" spirit and mope around for the rest of the day.

Precompetition hassles that are either beyond immediate control or not worth the emotional energy expenditure at that moment can also be "treed." That does not mean you will never deal with these issues. Rather it means you will set them aside for now because they are not helping you prepare, and you will deal with them at a more appropriate time.

When first using this procedure, you may find it helpful to act it out physically. For example, actually put your hand on the tree, or wall, or door, or boards around the rink while you think about letting the unwanted thought intrusions flow out of you into that object. Later it can be done symbolically or through imagery just by thinking about removing the intrusions. What may seem like a small, insignificant act can make a big difference in your feelings and performance.

Refocusing Before the Competition

One of the reasons you do not perform closer to your capacity all of the time is that you allow relatively unimportant thoughts, disturbances, or hassles to distract you. It is important to work on holding your best focus and on preventing little negatives from becoming major obstacles.

You have a few choices in dealing with an annoyance: You can let it keep bothering you, which doesn't make much sense; you can "tree it," which makes an infinite amount of sense for events beyond your control or for events you don't feel like dealing with right now; or you can deal with it now, which makes sense if it is within your control and if you feel like expending the necessary energy at the moment.

Let's say there is some organizational hassle that is beyond your control at the moment. It is beginning to bug you, and you would prefer that it not interfere with your competition preparation. Here's one possible solution: As soon as you feel the little bugging, before it gets too big, take a *deep breath,* and as you slowly exhale, say to yourself, "Relax . . . this is not within my immediate control. I don't like it; I would prefer that it wasn't happening, but it is not that *big* a deal. It doesn't *have* to bother me. It's not worth upsetting myself about it. "Tree it" in a vacant tree. The hassle doesn't *really* matter in terms of how I perform my skills, and that is why I'm here. Focus on something within your control such as what you want and plan to do: your warmup, positive imagery, competition preparations, music, controlled breathing, and so on.

One athlete says that whenever her performance is "off," she finds that before the competition she has "usually worried about external matters" that she couldn't change. We waste too much energy worrying about events that are beyond our immediate control (e.g., people being late for the bus, hassles on the morning of the competition, conditions at the competition site). Take, for example, the morning that preceded one athlete's worst competitive performance where "everything was a hassle and people were late." It was unfortunate that people did not show up on time, but at that point it was beyond her immediate control. Waiting for them might have been irritating, but it did not have to change the course of her day or life. As she said, "I let it control me. I let it influence a change in me."

How might she have dealt with the situation more constructively? She could have recognized and accepted her initial feelings of irritation, reminded herself that the situation was beyond her immediate control, and *shifted* her attention to something more constructive, something over which she had control. She could have told herself, for example, "Sit back in your seat in the bus . . .

breathe in—breathe out—*relax*. Conserve your energy." In this situation, you can remind yourself that if you are a few minutes late, it simply means that you have to be a little more organized at the competition site. Re-lax. Mentally review what you will do upon arrival. Close your eyes; use some imagery. Listen to a cassette tape. Before you know it, the people will arrive, the bus will leave and it won't really be that big a deal, will it? You would prefer that it didn't happen, but you can deal with it if it does, especially if you have a plan ready.

As this athlete pointed out, "Little things tend to bug you more because you are already keyed up, and you don't take the time to see them for what they really are." That's why it helps to have a preplanned procedure for dealing with such things; you need to keep them in perspective.

Another athlete mentioned that sometimes when she gets up in the morning on the competition day, she already knows "I'm not going to have a good day." The problem with that kind of "knowing" is that it can interfere with your potential, becoming a self-fulfilling prophecy. Because you already know that you won't perform well, you don't perform well. In essence your mind is telling your body that it will be "off" today and your body generally follows the instructions of your mind.

If you think you can't possibly have a good performance because you woke up feeling a little tired or because your warmup wasn't perfect, *keep it a secret* from your body. Your body won't know, and it will perform as it has been trained. Give your body a chance by avoiding or quickly shifting away from negative images, instructions, or expectations. It is particularly important that your final image before starting is helpful, *I can*, rather than harmful, *maybe I can't*. So if you find that you are about to use negative images or self-defeating instructions, instruct yourself to *stop*! as soon as you become aware of it. Replace the nonproductive images with reminders of your best performance focus, or give yourself positive, self-enhancing instructions. Practice *snapping back* into your preferred preevent focus.

Constructive refocusing applies to facing any difficult task or distraction as well as to self-motivation in training. Let's say you are at a training camp, you wake up, and it's raining for the third day in a row. Do you think, "Oh no, I don't want to train today!"? Or are you able to put the rain aside and refocus more positively, saying, "I've only got 2 weeks, and I'm going to make the best of every day"? You have the capacity to have a good performance *any* day, regardless of how you might initially feel in the morning. Do it once and you will prove it to yourself. Even if it feels like a not-so-good morning, and little things are upsetting you more than normal, remind yourself of the potential of your body.

Refocusing on You

Sometimes competitors can draw your focus away from where it is likely to do the most good. When this occurs, you need a way to bring it back. For example, the first time I saw the East German paddlers (the world leaders) compete at the world championships, I noticed several things. First, their kayaks and paddles were blue, which immediately set them apart from all other boats and made their athletes highly visible anytime they were on the water. A rumor was circulated that these special blue boats were made of some high-speed material that made them faster than all other boats, and the GDR did not allow people to get too close to them. These boats were never laying around unattended.

Off the water, even away from the competition site or in the hotel dining room, the East German athletes did not talk with people from other countries. They always moved in groups, separating themselves and giving an image of being larger than life. You *never* saw an East German athlete walking alone. When you saw their athletes striding towards you four or six abreast, they looked very powerful. Undoubtedly, there is power in numbers. Even at the banquet following the championships, they arrived as a team, sat at one table, stayed for a short time, and then all rose as a group and departed. Athletes from virtually all other countries were just beginning to celebrate when the East Germans left.

During training sessions the few days before the competition, they generally all dressed in the same distinct uniforms and often scheduled their training sessions so that they came off the water as other teams were just arriving—always trying to give the image of "first." This applied not only in training, but even in trailer setup and in getting boats on the trailer after the conclusion of the event. East German staff members often carried boats to and from the water and for postevent weigh-ins, whereas with other countries it was most often the athletes themselves who carried the boats.

A day or two before the competition, the other athletes would sometimes arrive at the training site and see several GDR coaches out in coach boats with watches, taking (or appearing to take) times as their athletes streaked across the water. The image that some of our athletes were left with was that they are machines—powerful performing machines—not people. They don't even party after winning the world championship. How can you beat that kind of machine?

I am not suggesting that we begin to duplicate the East German on-site behavior, but I am suggesting that we recognize and attempt to understand both the behavior and its intent. The entire demonstration can serve to intimidate competitors, and some of the East German's actions are probably designed to do so. The unwritten part of their preevent mental preparation is to buoy themselves up and sink other athletes, mentally, before the race starts. If others allow themselves to be distracted by these goings-on or begin to spend too much time focusing on the German athletes, imagining that they are invincible, the results can be disastrous.

However, if athletes are prepared for these conditions, recognize the intent of some of them, and have a refocusing plan to stay on track (following a personal plan of action—mental and physical), there should be no real problems. All athletes are made of the same flesh and blood and emotion, regardless of what might be allowed or not allowed to surface in public. All athletes can be beaten. But victory is only possible if attention is focused on appropriate and meaningful task cues rather than external, irrelevant matters.

Another example of a distraction occurred when Cerar, a Yugoslav gymnast who was the best in the world on the side horse for 11 years in a row, was about to win for the 12th time. Minutes before he started his routine, a Soviet gymnast walked over to him and asked him to explain how he performed an extremely difficult move that no one else had ever done in competition. As a result of the Soviet's preevent intervention, Cerar began to think about *how* he actually performed that move, both technically and mechanically. Then when he got to it in his routine, he missed it and for the first time he was defeated. He obviously did not expect that kind of distraction and the analytical focus it fostered; therefore, he did not have a refocusing plan to deal adequately with the distraction and resume a beneficial focus.

If he had developed a simple refocusing plan, perhaps beginning it as he chalked up his hands before mounting the apparatus, the results would likely have been different. For example, a simple clean run-through of his routine in imagery moments before he started might have set aside the technical thought and recreated the mental "feel" for a free-flowing performance.

Finding Your Own Space

In case you are distracted or experience some self-doubts, it is a good idea to establish a time at the competition site when you snap into your own space for your final psychological preparation, a time when you get ready to do what you have trained yourself to do. This time should be known, comfortable, and consistent, no matter where you are. The country, the competition site, the distractor, and in many cases the competitors are irrelevant.

At this point, even if hassles have occurred beforehand, you are now *here*. The past no longer matters; it is over. It might have been nice if everything up to this point had gone smoothly, but even if it didn't, you can't change that now. However, you can control your preparation procedure now. This is your time—*the time to get on track*.

In skiing, you can get on track as you sit back into the chair lift on the way up for your first run. At this point any turmoil, little problems, or worries can be "treed" and left behind at the bottom of the hill. Begin to see your potential by thinking about previous best performances, by drawing upon specific mental images, feelings, or memories of a particularly good performance, and by reminding yourself of what you must focus on to do well. Follow this with your basic preparation plan for the top of the hill, and when you leave that gate, go the way you know you can go.

Refocusing for Cultural Differences

When you live and compete under different cultural conditions, the attitude you take in and carry around with you is critical. The following suggestions for coping with cultural differences are applicable particularly in countries that do not have all the comforts to which North Americans are accustomed; they may be useful in helping you prepare to meet that challenge effectively.

- Treat your new environment as an adventure, a challenge, or a test of your ability to adapt, rather than complaining about feeling "trapped," talking about wanting to get out, or comparing things with the luxuries of home.

- Go in with a tolerant attitude. It may be a developing country with many problems. Roll with it or it will roll over you.
- Before you get off the plane, decide that you will look for the good parts, cope with the bad parts, and avoid complaining.
- People are not intentionally out to "get you." They are usually nice folks trying to do something they don't know much about, or they are simply following rules imposed upon them.
- Be prepared mentally for delays and cancellations. Develop a strategy for waiting. You will be doing a lot of sitting around, so bring cassettes, books, or anything else you find relaxing and enjoyable. Something as simple as picture-taking for ID cards may take a long time when there are 60 people waiting at once.
- Remember even though the food may not be great, you often will be eating much better than anyone else in the country. Bring food supplements. Carry in your own familiar goodies (e.g., peanut butter, chocolates, etc.). Anytime you are outside your residence, food can be a problem.
- Be prepared. Frequently there is no toilet paper anywhere.
- Internal transportation can be very difficult. Things do not run on time and are often cancelled.
- At major international events in developing countries, expect living conditions to be overcrowded compared with what you are used to. Four people to a room, crowded team dressing rooms, and limited space for equipment storage are not uncommon.
- Adherence to schedules is nonexistent. Expect confusion. You are bound to have organizational difficulties. You won't be able to find anyone who can make a decision. Everything is very slow or done at the last minute.
- In some areas there is a very good chance of delays in competition due to weather. Be prepared for postponements.
- Air pollution can be a real problem. Consider room air purifiers, especially if you have allergies.
- Once at your residence, you will have a lot of time to sit around. Weather and transportation delays mean even more waiting, so be prepared and bring some interesting things to enjoy such as audiotapes, videotapes, something to read, and table games.
- Paul Martini, 1984 world champion in pairs skating, offered the following advice: "Expect the absolute worst (in terms of con-

ditions) and you'll have a good time.'' You will also be better prepared to focus and refocus on what will allow you to perform best.

The major point that experienced Olympic coaches make is that once you start to focus too much time or energy on external hassles or on worrying about what is beyond your control, you are at a disadvantage. Your focus is best limited to your preparation for your own performance, to restful recreation, and to interesting diversions during the waiting periods—things over which you exert some control.

Through preplanning and good organization, you attempt to control what you can and accept or cope with what you can't. Team leaders should make every effort to change the critical things, but you should also recognize that some things can't be changed. Plan not to waste your physical and mental energy dwelling on them.

Refocusing at the Event

The finest performers seem to be able to look for advantages in every possible situation, even under what might normally be considered a less than ideal condition. They look for reasons why they should *still* be confident and optimistic.

In ski jumping, downhill skiing, or bobsleigh racing, your hearing good results such as a fast time for a previous competitor could be a distractor. It can also be turned to your advantage by thinking, "If he did that well, the course must be good and fast. I can do well, too."

In basketball a missed shot can be a distractor, but it can also be viewed in a positive light. Let's say you have a 90% shooting average from the floor. If you miss your first shot, you know the next 9 are going in. If you miss two or three in a row, you are sure to have a streak. The captain of Canada's gold medal basketball team at the 1983 World Student Games effectively used this strategy. If he missed a shot, he just thought of percentages. The more you miss, the surer you are the next 30 will go in. This is a much more constructive way of dealing with a missed shot than putting yourself down or telling yourself that you are off to a terrible start, either of which sets negative expectations for the remainder of the game.

Refocusing Within the Competition

For distractions, errors, or worries *within the event* the symbolic "tree it" concept discussed in the last chapter can be very effective. The moment you begin to get caught up in distractions, negative self-talk, worries about evaluation, or self-put-downs due to errors, remind yourself to "tree it." The negative focus or distraction will only hinder your performance. So set it aside for now and focus back on what is likely to help your performance. If you are angry and thinking about retaliation that might result in a penalty, "tree it" and refocus. If you're worried and thinking about an error in your routine or a competitor's good performance, "tree it" and refocus. Whenever you need to set aside a thought or feeling that is interfering or is likely to interfere with your performance, you can use the "tree it" concept. You might think of it as an automatic first step in your refocusing plan.

The term *park it*, a modern version of the "tree it" concept, has become a well-known and useful term for the basketball and hockey players with whom Canadian sport psychologist Cal Botterill has worked. Cal tells the story of one of the basketball players who had been "parking" quite a few thoughts in a row: official's bad calls, opponents' harassment, missed shots, and so on. After another questionable call, the athlete began to react, and the coach yelled, "Park it!" The player responded, "My lot's getting full, coach." In another incident, one of the hockey players was going through some strange gyrations and sounds. When the coach asked what he was doing, he replied, "I'm trying to park it, coach, but it's a big sucker."

Begin by "treeing" or "parking" small things at first, and then to move up to bigger things. It is easier to park a Volkswagen than a tractor-trailer until you become practiced at it.

Some athletes with whom I have worked have also become proficient at drawing "spirits" or energy from "parked" objects. For example, when one weight lifter made contact with the bar, he thought of the bar as radiating energy directly from the steel through him. Becoming highly activated and charged through this process, he perfected it to the point of simply focusing on the bar to get a surge of energy before his approach. A competitive paddler found that he was able to absorb energy in a similar way by gently squeezing his paddle while sitting in his kayak before the competition. Both of these athletes tied this energizing process into their precompetition plans.

If your competition focus plan is interrupted within the event, you need a way to snap back into your preferred focus as quickly as possible. A refocusing plan for use within the competition is a way of staying on top of things even under adverse conditions. This plan should break you away from unwanted distractions, negative thoughts, frustrations, or highly technical concerns and get you back into the "play," or refocus you on the specific task *you* want to accomplish. Your plan can also serve as a way of making things happen at opportune moments. If your competition focus plan is on all the way through the event, you will not need to use your refocusing plan, but in case problems should arise, have it ready.

The awareness of loss of ideal focus can sometimes signal refocus. To get back on track quickly, you need to know *in advance* what you are going to do, that is, how you are going to refocus. For example, in downhill skiing, awareness of "too much technical thought" might serve as the cue to focus "ahead" to the next gate. If you do not have a preplanned and practiced refocusing procedure, constructive refocusing *within* the competition will take too long. It will be all downhill, indeed.

In basketball, after a good play some players will lose focus by standing there admiring their shot instead of immediately getting back into the play. Let's assume you would prefer to shoot the ball and quickly get back into the play by running back down the court for defense. Your refocusing plan could be to shoot, to follow through, and then to immediately shift focus to your next task. The end of the follow-through itself can become a rapid-fire signal for whatever is desired—"run," "rebound," or "get back."

In another case, a player throws the ball away and then, while attempting to get the ball back, fouls the opposing player. Usually this occurs because the player is frustrated and "cannot get rid of the bad play." He or she can't "tree it" and get back into his or her position. In such a situation you first need to know what you should do on the court. Then develop and practice a plan to make that happen by using cues or cue words.

The captain of our women's university basketball team came to see me because of a refocusing problem. She wanted to have more control over a situation related to her role as an experienced player on an otherwise rookie basketball team. She was experiencing detrimental on-court frustration in response to her own play as well as to that of her somewhat inexperienced teammates. This frustrated feeling seemed to be totally uncontrollable during those games in which they were being soundly beaten. As she expressed it, "Once I realize we are losing a game, not due to the other team's skill but because of stupid errors on our part, I become more upset because I know all too well that we cannot expect to win as a team unless we are willing to play as a team."

Here are the thoughts that led her to a refocusing solution:

The only controllable circumstances within the situation are those that involve my personal play. I realize no matter how upset I get, I will never be able to control another's play. I realize also that I can control my own play. Hence, to take the situation in stride, I must govern my own play so that I am doing all I can to alleviate the pressure of losing during a game.

I am rather proud of my first refocusing strategy, primarily because I found it all on my own, and also because it works. One night as we were lined up by our bench, standing facing the scoreboard while the national anthem was being played, it came to me. I focused on the scoreboard, and below where the scores are indicated, I noticed an "Enjoy Coca-Cola" *sign, as big as life itself. That's when I said, ah-ha, that will be my cue. Since I'm always looking up to the scoreboard during the game, why not benefit from it! So, each time I felt frustrated (or more like swearing, and losing my cool) I'd look up and see* "ENJOY" *printed there as a reminder to, above all, enjoy myself. Even if the score indicated a trouncing, there would be the rest of the board, telling me it's all right—just* enjoy the game! *Much to my delight, this strategy, to this very day, is most effective.*

Perhaps the word *enjoy* helps athletes reconnect with the action in a more joyful, nonevaluative way, much as occurred when they first began their sport. The only adjustment I suggested for the basketball captain's refocusing strategy was to draw a happy face or write the cue word *enjoy* on her sneakers in case a scoreboard did not have her cue.

Interestingly, the concept of "play" or "enjoy" also seemed to be a good refocusing cue for members of the men's national basketball team. "Park it" (i.e., the frustration) and "play" seemed to get players back into the flow of the game. *Dance, boogie,* and *cook* are other terms used to symbolize "play," "enjoy," and "flow" that might be good refocusing cues or reminders for some athletes.

Larry Cain, 1984 Olympic canoeing champion, came up with a refocusing plan for problems in his race such as waves, wash, wallowing on wave, or a gust of wind. The cue was to "pick it up" or "break through it." As he said, "It's easier physically and psychologically to push through it when you first feel a blast of wind and then settle back down to pace than to slow down in the face of an obstacle—get behind—and then have to catch up to race pace and other racers. 'Attack' is better than 'defend' for obstacles within the race." Where two or more individuals must interact to compete, cueing must be simultaneous. In a crew boat about to be hit by a gust of wind, each team member would need to activate a collectively timed "pick up" or "break through it" cue, perhaps called out by one athlete.

One of our best singles kayakers often ran into problems if others pulled away from him in the first half of the race. If he let this "pulling away" grab his focus, and he began to worry about it, his race was virtually finished because he tended to "shut her down" and give up at that point. However, he had a very strong second half and had on occasion passed everyone after having been behind in the first half. If others began pulling away in the first half, his refocusing cue for "seeing the race slip away" became a flashback of him passing everyone in the second half of a strong race. When he was able to activate that flashback and combine it with thoughts like "stay on pace," "you're the strongest in the second half," "they'll die later," it could make all the difference in the race.

Dee Dee Haight, a highly skilled alpine skier, developed a plan to refocus within the race in case her focus drifted to outcome, evaluation, or the audience as it had done in the past. Her plan involved the use of the cue word *gate* and a shift of attention ahead to the next gate. The first time Dee Dee attempted this refocusing technique in the race, it worked partially but not fully. She was able to think of it *in* the race, which is an important first step, and it did get her back on track temporarily. However, her focus began to drift away in a short time within a couple of gates. Some possible solutions for this situation are presented on the next page.

- *Repetition*. What do you think would happen if during "drifting" conditions she was to continue to cue into "gate" every second gate? Would that hold her temporary focus all the way down the hill? Would it at least hold her focus away from personal or technical evaluation on the way down? It helped, but it did not create a complete and flowing connection for the duration of the course.
- *Alternate Cue*. It seems that her refocusing cue, "gate," was not intense enough to snap her into a lasting race focus. She was "sort of saying 'gate' but not *becoming* it"—not fully committing herself to it. We talked about the "time warp" concept which takes us from one dimension into another (in space exploration films). I suggested she try the cue word, *warp* and think of it as a way of entering another dimension. It provides a stronger image than "gate," and it's a better indication of what you are asking of yourself and committing yourself to do. You are not simply looking at the next gate; rather you are transforming yourself into another focus (e.g., a focus ahead, a gate focus) for the rest of the race. The time *warp* image aims to fully snap you into a speed dimension. When you think it, you think it with intensity and become that focus.
- *Practice*. It is important to practice refocusing whenever the opportunity arises and sometimes to create distracting situations in training so you become practiced at shifting dimensions. Set a few focusing goals for some training sessions. The goals might include such things as doing some free ski runs to get absorbed in the feeling of skiing without any technical evaluation; using some positive imagery in the chair lift on the ride up for the next run; practicing shifting focus on the way down—from a technical (precision) focus to another dimension such as "looking ahead" free from technical evaluation. Of course, you must also practice entire runs free of technical evaluation.

Olympic skier Karen Stemmle told me that her preferred race focus during the race is "totally on what I'm doing at that moment and what is coming up next"—that is, present awareness but future focus. In her worst races her focus was often where it was least effective—behind her. She dwelled on past mistakes, thinking about "an almost fall" or about saving herself "from dying" rather than on "going fast." Clearly these are performance-defeating thoughts that did not help her achieve her goal. What she needed was a preplanned way to snap back into her preferred race focus, *quickly*.

One of the best approaches in such circumstances is to "tree" the past, put it aside for now. She cannot control the past, but the *focus ahead* is within her immediate control. In case she got caught up in worrying about a past error on the way down the hill, I asked her to think of a strategy to *shift* her focus into another dimension, such as a speed dimension, to think of a cue or cue word to help her refocus on the spot, and to practice it. Negative or self-defeating thoughts became a signal to *zap* back into her best race focus (e.g., to the feel of her body, to the focus ahead).

Refocusing After the Event

Often it is helpful to refocus after an event. Dwelling on past poor results is as unproductive as dwelling on occurrences earlier in the competition. You cannot change what happened. However, you can and should gather the necessary information from your experience. Then, move on to the present and act upon what is within your control.

Refocusing With a Remaining Event

One of the most dramatic examples of the importance of collective refocusing after an event occurred at the 1983 World Championships in canoeing. A crew of four had just failed to make the finals in the 1,000-meter event, which had been their major goal for that year. When they came off the water, paddles were flying, heads were bowed, spirits had bottomed out. However, there still remained a semifinal race in another event that afternoon and, if they qualified in that event, a finals race the following day.

Coach Denis Barré, the four paddlers, and I sat down after the setback and talked about what went well, what was off, and what needed to be altered for the afternoon race. Denis asked each athlete to express his feelings about what had transpired in the race. It was a beautiful experience to share because the athletes were so open. First, athletes expressed their feelings: "I blew it," "went too hard too early,'' ''was out of stroke,'' and so on. Then they made suggestions for improvement. The coach supported the following italicized suggestions:

- We didn't feel fully ready at the start.—*Do an additional start in warm-up* (i.e., 3 starts).
- We were spinning our wheels trying to stay with the East Germans on our right and Soviets on our left.—*Stick with your own race plan: make sure you have a pause in the stroke once you hit race pace* (i.e., have a ''pause'' checkpoint at a specific place on the course); and *hold your own pace and start kick point a little earlier.*

We sat there on the ground next to the boat house and talked for about an hour after the race. Everyone else had left. When we finally went back to the hotel for lunch, those athletes were in a totally different spirit from when they came off the water. They were optimistic, they were ready, they had a definite plan which drew upon the errors they had made that morning. The ride back to the hotel was high and positive.

I felt that the coach had done a super job at drawing out what needed to be drawn out. The only thing I did at the end of that meeting was to put the action-oriented content into point form to serve as a clear reminder of what they could do to improve their performance for the afternoon:

- Do the same warm-up but with 3 starts.
- Have a prerace reminder to race *your* race.
- Use a ''pause'' checkpoint.
- Start your ''kick'' earlier.

The coach later wondered aloud, ''What should I say when they leave the dock this afternoon?'' I suggested that he simply remind them to focus on what they had to do, that is, follow the race plan. That afternoon that crew made the finals—the first time a Canadian crew ever made the finals in that event—and the following day they placed fifth in the world.

I feel quite certain that that meeting had a significant effect on their refocusing and on their subsequent performance. Before the meeting they were feeling down, frustrated, angry, and cheated. Without a refocusing session to express some of those feelings and to get back on track, it is very likely that some of them would have hung on to those negative feelings for the remaining event and would not have performed to potential.

This experience, along with a few others similar to it, have clearly brought out the advantages of talking and refocusing after an event, especially after a poor performance when another event remains. With this crew, every time we have spoken after a poor performance about what went well, what was off, and what to refocus on, the next races have been "on." They seem to race best when they make sure the race focus plan is fresh in their minds before the start of the race. One member of this crew said to me, "The group is unique because we can communicate; people will express what they are feeling." For teams, communication is important for collective focusing and refocusing. We need to work more on this in virtually all groups.

Refocusing After the Completion of a Poor Competition

If you have a poor result, fill out the Postcompetition Evaluation form (see Appendix A), look for anything that went well, look for what was off in the preevent procedure as well as in the event focus plan, and make a mental note of what needs to be done for improvement. Then forget about the result. Let it go: "Tree It." That competition is history and is beyond your control. The only thing within your control is what you choose to tie into your plan for the next competition. There is no advantage in wasting time or energy dragging yourself down. You have done what you can do; you have drawn the constructive lessons out of that event and now you move on. Shift your focus, think positive thoughts, imagine positive things, remind yourself what you did well today, remind yourself of your personal track record, your best competitions, your capacity, your future goals.

Developing Your Own Refocusing Plan

The personal plans you make or don't make and the self-talk or focus you engage yourself in before and during competitions all have a critical effect on your performance. If you can get into the right frame of mind *before the event*, and stay focused *within the event*, things will flow. If you would prefer not to get worried about or bothered by little things, if you want to stay positive, up, and focused on the good results and happenings, then devise a plan to *do it*. If you think you need to forget poor results and be more positive, instead of dragging yourself down, then work on a refocusing plan for negative intrusions, and act on it.

Think about the situations you have faced that have resulted in unwanted distractions or detrimental reactions. Think about the times when you could have benefitted from being able to regain control quickly. List these situations and others that are likely to occur, and next to each, outline a refocusing strategy that has already worked or might work for you.

Use the Refocusing Planning sheets in Appendix A, and draw from the examples outlined in this book, as well as from your own experience, for appropriate refocusing strategies to try. Then practice them. As you can see by reading these plans, the specific concerns and strategies for refocusing are different for different athletes. You must develop and refine the individualized plan that is most effective for *you*!

Dee Dee Haight's and Larry Cain's refocusing plans presented in Tables 7.1 and 7.2 provide examples of completed plans.

Table 7.1 Refocusing Plan for Dee Dee Haight (Alpine Skiing)

Preevent hassle
- Let the coaches or other personnel figure out and rectify the problem or hassle, not my department.
- If that fails, try to rectify the situation or deal with it as best as possible.
- Turn what may have been a negative into a positive.
- Use the adrenaline or anger as a positive and extra advantage rather than bringing me down.

Delay in start
- Don't dwell on the delay and what will happen.
- Don't worry that this or that will happen because the race is delayed.
- Relax, think of anything and everything that makes me happy.
- Don't worry that I'm not turning gray with worry or guilt because I'm not upset.

(Cont.)

Table 7.1 Cont.

Loss of ideal focus in race run
- As course was inspected in 'sections,' deal with the mistake as a mistake in the previous section; thus, with the entrance into the "new section," a refocusing occurs.
- Think and deal with the remainder of the course as previously rehearsed and planned in inspection (i.e., get to the bottom, let it go, next gate).

Mistake in race run
- Deal with mistake, as I would a loss of focus.
- Go for the future versus the past.

Poor performance—first run
- Think of second run with a "nothing to lose attitude."
- Deal with what went wrong in the first run and treat the second as a new run with nothing to lose; again, don't dwell on the past.

Poor performance—final run
- Determine what went wrong and why. Learn from the mistake, train and see the mistake dissolve mentally and physically.
- Make the poor performance a challenge to defeat.

Other areas
- If a series of races or events have been going incorrectly (1 to 2 weeks), sit back, refocus on what I need and want, and how to get there. Determine why the things have been going wrong. Be analytical. Associate and do things for me that make me feel good. Put things into perspective; write it on paper. Look at it from an "outsider's" point of view.

Table 7.2 Refocusing Plan for Larry Cain (Canoeing)

Preevent hassle

Plan 1 (ideal)
- Avoid prerace hassle.
- Isolation from others and/or potential hassle.

Plan 2
- Turn and walk away from problem.
- Use relaxation tape or listen to relaxing music (get heart rate down, feel relaxed arms and legs). Perhaps also a few long deep breaths.

(Cont.)

Table 7.2 Cont.

- Refocus on race plan.
- After relaxation, draw upon anger from hassle for *controlled energy*. [Author's comment: I'm not sure you need to recall the anger, as the goal itself will be enough to charge you for the event. However, if a little anger is left over it could be used as a possible flash for energizing.]

Delay in start
- Not likely.
- Listen to relaxing music.

False start
- No problem; circle and do it again like practice.
- Past experience has been that I gain confidence because I know after doing well on the start once, it is going to be "easy" the second time.

Nonideal conditions
(Wind, waves, motor boat wash, wind gust)

Plan 1 (ideal)
- *Anticipate* condition and problem.
- *Attack-pound* through it, keeping boat speed and concentration flow.
- Settle into pace after.

Plan 2 (contingency)
- If rhythm is broken, concentrate on boat movement and technique.
- Think of perfect catch and pull;
- Feel boat lift out of water again.
- Cue word—*lift* or *jump*.

Poor start (crooked start)
Currently, I am practicing starts in all conditions. Ideally, I don't have a problem. First think about setting up perfectly. If I have problems, I plan to correct them by perfecting techniques to straighten boat. A more intense focus should eliminate or lessen degree of problem.

Other areas (strong finish)
- What do you think about refocusing on the last 100 to 150 meters as a new race? [Author's comment: I like it. It makes a lot of sense to me for reenergizing mentally and then physically.]
- Narrow focus to only finish line and power—deep crisp strokes.

Implementing the Plans

I f you have acted upon the suggestions in the previous four chapters of this book, you now have a psychological plan to practice. You also, perhaps for the first time, have a specific goal for psychological skill development, and that goal is to refine your plan and use it for the first competition of the year. The adaptation of the plan into a highly refined and useful tool will come through using it. With "doing," you will discover very quickly what is working, as well as what needs work, adaptation, or elimination.

Once the precompetition plan, the competition focus plan, and the refocusing plan have been developed, the entire plan should be sufficiently practiced before competition so that in competition it can unfold in a fluid way, without worry or distraction. When time trials, simulated competitions, or scrimmages occur, you should treat them as actual competitive events so that you have an opportunity to practice the entire on-site competition plan from warm-up to refocus. You should experience the plan in a simulated competition and then adapt it as desired before attempting to use it in a competitive event.

Through simulations, you can practice and refine your preevent mental and physical warm-up, your within-event focus, and your refocusing skills. In simulations a countdown to the start should occur just as it will unfold in a competition. The order of events, competitive demands, and distractions should be simulated as closely as possible through contrived situations, role playing, or imagery.

Before you use a plan in a vitally important competition, you should test it and refine it, if necessary, in a less important competition. For example, use it in a local or regional competition before the Nationals; use it in an international tour before using it in the World Championships or Olympic Games. This will allow you to become more practiced at using the plan. The plan will either be working as is, or it will require slight refinement. In either case, as a result of using the plan, you can enter the more important competition with additional confidence: "I have a solid mental preparation plan and it's already worked" or "I have a well-developed mental preparation plan and it's been refined to work even better."

In the area of mental training outlined in this book, almost everything that you want to accomplish can be tied into your regular on-site training and competitive program. That is the best way to ensure it's getting done. Next week, for example, as part of your general warm-up for training, you can include a small part of your preferred preplanned precompetition warm-up (physical and mental). In subsequent training warm-ups you can try half of it, most of it, and then all of it. You can also begin practicing your preferred race, game, or event focus while performing certain skills in training. At first you might attempt this for a short period of time and then gradually work up to holding the desired focus longer.

The ultimate goals of practice are (a) to hold the preferred focus, (b) to hold it for all important skills which relate to the game, race, or event, and (c) to hold it for the entire training session. As important as it is to maintain your preferred focus in practice, it is often useful to introduce distractions into your training sessions in order to practice your refocusing plans. These plans should be practiced *anytime* you are distracted or lose focus, whether in the sport environment or not. Psychological skills are valuable tools in all life situations.

Time Frame

My personal observations tell me that it takes from 1 to 3 years for an athlete to get his or her psych plan refined enough to affect performance *consistently*. Of course, there are many exceptions. During the first year, most athletes increase their awareness and understanding of how the psych functions, and needs to function, in competition. As athletes experiment and refine their plans, much personal growth occurs, and their psych plans come together beautifully for *some* competitions.

Athletes who have approached their mental game in a serious and persistent way during the first year begin the second year with a much improved understanding of themselves relative to competition. They are in a better position to *act* upon their mental plans and to make slight refinements when necessary. I have noticed that preevent readiness, event focus, and general ability to remain positive and to cope become much more consistent during the second year of mental training. Performance also becomes more consistent. By the third year, assuming the athletes have committed time and energy to systematically developing psychological skills, the mental plans really begin to make a difference.

How far and how quickly *you* move along the mental control continuum depends upon where you start and how much you focus on improving.

Albert Ellis outlined three steps to self-control that have been adapted for your use.

1. *Resolution*. Fill out the Competition Reflection form and resolve to do something to improve your mental skills.
2. *Action*. Develop your own mental plans for precompetition, competition, and refocusing; put those plans into action.
3. *Persistence*. Continue to implement, evaluate, and refine your plans over time.

Persistence seems to define when, or whether, you will arrive at your desired destination.

Olympic Reflections

I worked with the Canadian National Canoe Team for 3 years before the 1984 Olympic Games and introduced them to the same basic mental training program that I have presented to you in this book. In the 1984 Olympic Games, those athletes made the finals in 10 out of the 12 events and won medals in 6 of them: 2 gold, 2 silver, and 2 bronze. As a team they achieved the performance goals they had established several years earlier, although there were a couple of instances in which athletes did not perform to full potential.

In the view of most of the athletes and coaches on the team, the mental training program was successful in helping them perform to potential under-high stress conditions. In my view, those athletes who were most receptive to the program and who committed themselves to it seriously for 3 years were the ones who gained most, exhibited most self-control, and performed closest to potential in the 1984 Olympic Games. They knew exactly what they had to do to perform best, they knew what to focus on, and they were completely confident that if they followed their focus plan, they would perform well. Their well-established preevent plans held distractions to a minimum, and they knew how to handle distractions if they did arise. In almost all cases, the most highly skilled athletes were among the most receptive to approaching the mental training program conscientiously. You do not have to be highly skilled for this program to work for you; you do have to be highly committed, which was a common characteristic of these athletes.

Olympic Development

Reflecting back on those 3 years, this is what seems to have transpired. The first year provided an orientation to mental training and resulted in some basic mental plans and an increase in self-awareness relative to competitive performance. By the latter part of the second year, the prerace plans and race plans were well established and in most cases refined and working well. During the third year, emphasis was placed on the fine tuning of athletes' plans, on improving athletes' skills at refocusing, and on generating more team harmony.

By the end of the third year, the overall capacity to refocus in the face of obstacles or setbacks was surprisingly good, as evidenced by the team's reaction when we arrived at the L.A. airport. We went through accreditation quickly but then unexpectedly had to wait in the airport for several hours for a bus. This wait extended over the lunch hour. Our athletes could easily have slipped into a negative frame of mind and dwelt on their discomfort. Yet the athletes handled the situation well, not happy about it, but also not wasting energy worrying. I noticed only one young athlete grumbling, which he quickly stopped when I reminded him that it wasn't worth wasting energy over.

Team harmony went from an all-time low at the first Olympic training camp to an all-time high at the final training camp just before the Olympic Games. The atmosphere drastically changed—from one where some people constantly complained about other athletes, coaches, and administrators to one that was quite pleasant. Initially, there was no real sense of team, and in some cases people even hoped that other team members would not do so well. In the end, caring was genuine and everyone really pulled for everyone else.

A large part of this change came from raising the issue with the team, asking every team member what could be done to improve team harmony, and circulating their suggestions to the group. Most of all, individual athletes made personal commitments to try to get along better, and it worked.

Two of the athletes who impressed me most were Olympic gold medalists Larry Cain and Alwyn Morris. Although they are different in many ways and come from extremely different cultural backgrounds, they were very similar with respect to the incredible intensity and quality they brought to training. Other athletes trained hard, but these two always set the pace. They were already faster in their events, yet they still worked harder than the others. They always brought to training an extremely high quality of effort, which is a distinction they share with world leaders in other sports. I can recall days when Alwyn trained with a splitting headache and still pushed himself to the limit and drew from the well. "Did we train as hard as the East Germans today? If not, we are one step behind. Did the Soviets take the day off? Not likely!"

At any time during the year, Larry could tell you exactly how many training days were left before the World Championships or the Olympic Games. He looked forward to training hard every day and could hardly wait for the big competition to arrive. For 2 years prior to the 1984 Olympic Games, whenever I handed out forms to be completed, Larry would sign them, "Larry Cain 1984 Olympic Champion" and then would list his events. He even signed some of his university papers this way. Larry was always the first person to hand in his mental plans—prerace plan, race focus plan, and refocusing plan—and always the first to complete his race evaluation forms, which he did religiously without prompting. Athletes who are committed to developing effective plans and who are persistent in refining them reap the most benefits.

Sue Holloway and Alexandra Barré, the first Canadian women ever to win an Olympic medal in the sport of canoeing, also impressed me with their ability to develop and follow a detailed race plan and to push their limits when they needed to most. Just before their Olympic final, as we walked down the long gray dock carrying Sue and Alexandra's boat to the water, Sue shattered the tension by joking, "This is like walking to your own execution. I hope the governor gives me a reprieve." We all laughed.

As they got in the boat, the final word uttered to them was, "Just follow your race plan and push your limits . . . push the 10." They paddled a super race, following their plan and pushing the 10, and won an Olympic silver. Bronze had been their realistic goal, gold their dream goal. The only other time I recall them both completely extending themselves was at the 1983 World Championships when they cracked an important confidence barrier by beating the strong Soviet crew for the first time. If you hope to touch your dream, you must follow your plan and plan to extend yourself.

Olympic Refocusing

At the 1984 Games Hugh Fisher and Alwyn Morris had the goal of two gold medals. However, in their first final, the 500-meter pairs kayak race, they did not effectively carry out their transition to race pace and ended up third. They were emotionally "down" on the victory podium and still remorseful several hours later. I went to their room and asked how they were doing. I wanted to know if they had been able to put the race aside and start refocusing on tomorrow's race. One had been able to do so, one had not.

I was probably more direct with them than ever before. "It does you no good to punish yourself about this morning's race. It's finished. You can't control history. If you set it aside now and begin to focus on tomorrow's race, which is within your control, you can walk out of here with a bronze medal and a gold medal. I know your goal was two Olympic golds, but a bronze and a gold is not bad. Better than a bronze and *nothing*. You are capable of doing it. You can punish yourself and mope around, or you can get back on track and do what you came here to do." We sat there in silence for a while, with me wondering whether I had been talking to a blank wall. But that's all I had to say. The rest was up to them.

I noticed at supper they were beginning to interact, ever so slightly letting the outside in, and later there was more interaction and even some humor in their room. I felt relieved. The crisis had passed and I felt they would be on track. The next morning they had a super race. They were very much in control of the race and of the gold medal they had been seeking. They broke the previous Olympic and world record by 2 seconds (over 1,000 meters). Sometimes you need to remind yourself to lighten up in order to refocus and get back on track. I later found out that Alwyn had dived to the bottom of the pool next to where we were staying, touched bottom, and left the misery of that first race down there. He "pooled" it.

CHAPTER 9

Assessing the Plan

I n order to evaluate psychological plans, you need to put yourself into the real situation. However, without a basic plan and a commitment to evaluate and refine the plan, experiencing the real situation will not necessarily lead to the desired improvements. You may compete numerous times and continue to be overly worried before the event or repeatedly distracted within the event. It is important to develop and implement a plan, and it is equally important to evaluate and refine the plan.

The evaluation phase is critical and ongoing. After every competition, take the time to reflect upon what happened before the event and within the event. Did your warm-up work? Did it hold your attention? Did it help you feel ready? Did your preevent reminders help you to focus appropriately? What specifically seemed to help? What might still be improved upon?

Did your event focus plan work? Go through your game or event section by section. Were you able to hold your preferred focus? If you lost your best focus, were you able to plug in cue words at appropriate times to get back on track? Did they help? Would another cue be better?

When your performance "falls apart," it usually falls apart in your head before it reaches your body. Why is your performance in one race or one quarter better than in another? Most often because you approach it differently *in your head*. If you were "off" on something, for example, if you didn't anticipate or were not assertive enough, it is important to assess where your focus was at that time. Then you may ask, Where should it have been? Postcompetition evaluations allow you to become more aware of these discrepancies and thereby place you in a better position to improve segments of your performance as well as your overall performance.

Postcompetition Evaluation

You can gain a great deal by setting aside time for self-assessment after all wins and losses. One of the best ways to do this is through the Postcompetition Evaluation forms in Appendix A. These forms help you to go back and look at what might have aided or hindered your performance. They allow *you* to examine your own performance to learn as much as possible from that performance and to clearly discover the mental patterns (e.g., thinking, focus, activation) related to your best and not-so-best performances.

The form should be filled out after competitions, on-site if possible, and later reviewed. Use the longer form until you are very sure of the patterns related to your very best performances and your not-so-great performances. Then you can switch to the short form.

Part of what you decide to work on to improve your performance should be based on knowing where the real problem lies. For example, why go back and rework only physical skills that are already highly refined when it is fairly obvious from the postcompetition evaluation that the problem was a loss of focus, of dealing with distractions, or of controlling activation?

When performance problems surface in competitions, it makes sense to assess what happened inside your head and to work on that in conjunction with your physical skills. Pay attention to refining the strategies that will help you to deal effectively with distractions before and during your performance. Assess your self-talk, your event focus, and your ability to refocus within the event. Refining these strategies will lead to improving the mental state that likely resulted in the performance problem.

After a poor performance or a loss, some of you may not want to fill out a Competition Evaluation form. However, competitions and setbacks are unique and wonderful learning opportunities. You really should take full advantage of them. To get back on track quickly and to learn the most from that not-so-super experience, assess your preparation and performance regardless of how painful you initially think it might be. It may help to remember that your goal is not to dwell on these experiences, but to learn from them. Only from understanding what occurred in particular competitive experiences can you develop a plan to decrease the likelihood of similar negative experiences.

A day or two after the competition (or in some cases between games), reread your completed evaluation form, thinking about what you should attempt to do or avoid doing at the next competition. If you have any changes that you feel would be helpful, tie them into your next precompetition plan or competition focus plan. If you run through the change a few times in your imagery and practice it during the week, you will have a better chance of implementing it in the next competition. Whenever there is some training time before the next competition, you can benefit from thinking about ways to best focus *during training* to achieve the proper focus for the next competition.

One athlete decided to stop filling out the Postcompetition Evaluation form because she felt she was thinking too much about what she was thinking. She wanted to just *do* it and not *think* about it (i.e., just go fast). Perhaps you will also have this feeling. You need to spend enough time evaluating your competition focus to know what works best for you. Once that is clear, you no longer have to think so much about what you were thinking. Just focus on doing what you know makes you go best.

Still, the need for some sort of regular postevent evaluation is never *completely* eliminated, even though it may become more informal. You cannot expect to attain and maintain *consistent* high-level performance without evaluating those mental factors that have the greatest influence on your performance: your pre-competition thinking, your competition focus, and your refocusing.

The postcompetition evaluation is aimed at improving the *consistency* of high-level performance. If you are satisfied with inconsistent performance, for example, coming close to your potential every now and then, the Postcompetition Evaluation forms are probably not so crucial. If you are not satisfied with inconsistent performances, then I invite you to use the forms.

Filling Out Evaluation Forms

The Competition Evaluation forms provided in Appendix A outline an important process that has helped many high-performance athletes to refine and strengthen their psych plans. Give the forms a chance to work for you. Use them to evaluate your overall feelings and focus and also use them as a reminder of how you should focus for best results. Fill out these forms after at least three or four consecutive competitions. Then sit down with the forms in front of you and go over them, looking closely for differences between best and not-so-best performances. Your objective is to discern clearly what kind of focus works most effectively for you.

Continue to use the Postcompetition Evaluation forms for as long as they seem to contribute something to the refinement of your plan and performance. That will differ for different athletes. Some athletes gain from using this kind of assessment form after all major events, while others prefer to include their postcompetition reflections in their diaries. This practice is an acceptable option as long as comments about mental state (e.g., feelings and focus) and how it seemed to affect performance are included. If you choose to write your reflections in your diary, be sure to include your responses to what you feel are the most important questions on the Competition Evaluation form.

After using the evaluation forms several times, some athletes prefer to individualize the forms, drawing out only the most relevant items. Some prefer to review the event in their own heads, for example, by reflecting upon how well they held their best focus during the event. Others prefer to draw out the lesson by talking over the event with their coach. If you reach a point where you feel you have gained everything you can from the forms, then stop using them. But continue to evaluate your preparation and performance in some way.

Each of the above assessment procedures has the same objective: to help you draw the positive lessons from the experience so that you become more consistent in your best feelings, focus, and performance. What is important here is for you to develop the habit of self-monitoring, so that you are able *to act* constructively upon your own assessment and input.

Once you know what focus works best, write it in big letters and stick it up on your wall. Then simply remind yourself of that focus or attempt to recall that feeling before the start of your event. If something does go wrong, think back to that big sign on your wall. Reflect back on what you did in your best performance(s). Attempt to carry that feeling and that focus into your next event.

Learning From History and Unmet Goals

One thing I've always wanted to be able to do is to fly, freely and unassisted like a bird; the other is to control history. Wouldn't it be wonderful to be able to step back and reverse some aspects of history? I still have hopes of flying unassisted, but I have come to accept that there is no effective strategy for controlling the past. History is beyond our control, so the best we can do is learn from it.

In attempting to learn from our personal experiences, it is important to distinguish between what is potentially within our control and what is not. One is a legitimate and constructive area upon which to focus, the other is a waste of energy.

At the 1983 World Canoe Championships held in Tampere, Finland, the Canadian team (with few exceptions) did not perform to potential. Environmental conditions had a lot to do with it. On the day of the finals, heavy headwinds and waves faced all paddlers in the outside lanes, yet relatively little wind was encountered in the protected inside lanes. Our athletes consistently drew the outside lanes.

After the event I heard the following comments from two of our best athletes: "I wasted the year . . . I did all that work for nothing"; "We got the icing [one bronze medal], but no cake [2 gold medals]"; "You wonder if it's worth it, all that preparation and then it's blown down the drain by a bad lane."

I was a part of that team and shared in their disappointment. In addition to the unfair wind disadvantage on the outside lanes, we sustained a broken footrest at the start of the women's K-4 (teamboat race), and after Alwyn Morris led all the way to the final lap in the 10,000-meter singles kayak race, he was hit by another boat and finished the race well back, with a cracked paddle sustained in the collision.

I wondered about the comment, "I wasted the year." In a sense it was true in terms of the final goal for that year (e.g., gold medals in the World Championships). Would I then also have been accurate in saying that I wasted the year in working with this team because my overall goal was to help them reach their goal? Perhaps so. But most of them gained something over the year in terms of their mental preparation and the organization of their race plans. Most of them entered the event in good spirits and with good basic strategies. Most of the team performed very well until the winds came. In fact, more reached the finals than ever before. In addition, most athletes learned something important from this event. So perhaps it was a waste of time in terms of medals and primary goals, but other goals were achieved, and still others remained to be achieved, which were, in fact, achieved the following year at the Olympic Games.

In an attempt for all of us to draw the most out of the lessons from that event, I distributed a questionnaire to each athlete. I did this while we were on the bus to the airport and requested that they return it *before* we returned to Canada. The following questions were posed:

1. Could *you* have done anything different to have been better prepared for the conditions that confronted you here at Tampere? If so, what?
2. Could the *coaching staff* or any of the support staff, including medical doctor and sport psych consultant, have done anything different to help you be better prepared for the conditions you faced here? If so, what?
3. In terms of your preparation and race plan, list suggestions event by event for improvement that might help for the next year's performance at the Olympics.

When I reviewed the responses of our two strongest athletes, Larry Cain and Alwyn Morris, both of whom won Olympic gold the next year, it became clear that they, more than any other athletes on the team, felt that as individuals they could have done something different to be better prepared. They assumed personal responsibility for their destiny. They did not attribute blame to the coaching or support staffs for not having done something better to prepare them for the conditions faced. They did not look to the weakness or inaction of others as a possible excuse for their performance. They learned a great deal from the experience and drew out exactly what they had to do personally in order to prepare for that condition and any other tough conditions in the future. They did not miss anything in terms of the lesson, and they did not wait around for others to draw it out for them. They seemed to know that the only way to be sure that the lesson is learned and acted upon is if one takes the responsibility to do it oneself. And they did just that.

Athletes' suggestions for improvements to help the following year's performance at the Olympics included the following:

- Use a different plan for headwind, work on the headwind technique.
- Train for more confidence in strength in this situation (did not feel prepared to deal with wind).
- Plan more definite workouts in days immediately before races (i.e., I would prefer a definite plan for the week or two of training before the Worlds or Olympics—right up to the start, especially the day or two before).
- Do workouts in bad weather conditions.
- Build in flexibility in race plan.
- Be mentally prepared regardless of race conditions, face up to it.
- Train in conditions similar to those we will face.
- Simulate conditions; it's difficult not to be affected by the conditions if you rarely encounter them.
- Practice time trials in various wind conditions and a little more practice in wavy conditions; in our case we should train more in headwinds by adapting our stroke for longer water time and less air time).
- Train on a course consistently, regardless of conditions, to match race conditions.
- Keep a boat (crew) together for a more lengthy time.
- Race tough competition.
- Concentrate a little more on following the race plan (especially during the race itself).
- Employ more mental rehearsal or visualization.
- Realize that coaches can't do much to help us at the competition site in such conditions; however, they can help us prepare for them beforehand in training.

Consider Larry Cain's comment.

(For the 500 meter) I'd like to take the races I have inside me and build on them with regard to the last 150 meters. I could walk away with a race with a super finish; (for the 1,000 meter) I'd like to lower my 250

splits further but maintain an even pace per 250 meters. The points of the race which are the most important, I feel, are the 500- to 600-meter part and the last 150 meters. A more intense, powerful effort here could blow the race wide open for me.

One of the main reasons that these and many other athletes excel is that they have become very proficient at self-assessment, at self-monitoring, and at drawing the important lessons out of their experiences. As you become more practiced at this process, you too will be able to move closer to your potential.

Consistency and Confidence

Confidence affects results. Results also affect self-confidence. To improve confidence and the consistency of results, you can make use of simulation training and work on the consistency of thoughts and focus going into competitions. The consistency of thoughts before competitions and the consistency of an appropriate focus within a competition directly affect the consistency of results and, in turn, self-confidence. Both can be developed through simulation training and mental planning.

Enhancing Self-Confidence

One reason that exceptionally talented athletes sometimes lack complete confidence in their abilities is a tendency to cling to, or revert back to, a less talented self-image, one that was probably accurate for a long time. For example, on the way up, you were relatively less skilled than now. Now that you have become highly skilled, a less skilled self-image is no longer accurate. Yet when things are not going so well, when performance is inconsistent in hassle situations or in high-stress situations, you are likely to regress to that self-image.

It is important to recognize and accept that your image of your less talented self is no longer valid. Your ability is a proven reality. Your *ability* does not change from one event to the next. Your confidence in or acceptance of that ability, your precompetition thinking, and your focus of attention may change, but your *ability* does not suddenly change. It remains with you.

When you find yourself doubting your ability, think about your best performances and your victories. Think in an objective and rational way about your own capacity to perform. Often this kind of reflection is best done in a calm time away from the competitive setting. Think about the real-world proof that demonstrates that you do have the ability—for example, the training sessions and competitions in which you broke through barriers. You could not have had those performances unless you were an exceptional athlete with exceptional ability.

Your performing well, even occasionally, means that you have the *ability* to perform well. You have done it. If you were truly incapable of performing that well, you could not have performed at that level even once. Accept this kind of basic thinking about your talents and abilities; it will help you to *avoid* or reduce self-defeating thoughts on the competition day.

Once you have developed a precompetition plan and a competition focus plan that draws upon what has already worked best for you, you have even more reason to go into competitions with added confidence. One Olympic athlete told me that before her worst performances she didn't feel confident enough. I asked her, *"What do you do or say to yourself* that leaves you feeling confident in one performance and not confident in the next?" The poor performance situation surfaced when she either had a bad warm-up or got up feeling tired.

Neither of these conditions has to affect performance negatively. A warm-up is a warm-up; a competition is quite another matter. You have had, on occasion, a less than perfect warm-up and still had a good performance. And feeling tired in the morning does not have to affect a performance negatively. You can be half asleep in the morning and still become highly activated, highly charged, immediately before the event, which is when you need your high activation. You have probably woken up feeling sluggish on some occasion and still had a great day of training or competing.

Remind yourself that you have performed extremely well under less-than-ideal conditions, even if it was only on a few occasions, so you know you are *capable* of doing it. Stop looking for proof that you aren't that good, and start looking for proof that you are.

Richard Bach pointed out that if you "argue for your limitations, sure enough they're yours." Instead of looking for reasons why you might perform poorly, look for reasons why you can perform well. Instead of searching your history to support a belief that you aren't good under certain conditions, start looking for proof that you *are* good under *any* conditions. Look for proof in the real world to demonstrate your abilities to yourself. Commit yourself to doing that. If you look, you will find. You are not asking yourself to do anything unreasonable—only to perform like you can perform. Let your past history, along with your present thinking and images, support your ability and your feelings about what you *can* do. If you have a physical advantage such as strength or conditioning, try to apply it mentally. For example, remind yourself that because of this strength you can "push it" more. This might help you to "push the limit" and give you a reason for believing that you can do it.

Sometimes training with the best is a good way to enhance your belief in yourself. One of Canada's world record holders in swimming said, "Earlier in my sport career I was not really confident. I didn't think I was good until I went to an American college with the best athletes in the world and realized I'm just as good as these guys."

Performance is rooted in expectations and beliefs. A French kayaker who won a silver medal at the 1980 Olympics told a similar story. Compared with other elite paddlers, he was not very big, but he had excellent talent. He never fully believed in himself, nor had he excelled at the international level until he trained for a couple of months with one of the best teams in Europe. At that point he *knew* he could do it. By paddling with some previous Olympic medalists and staying with them in training, he secured an absolute belief in himself. As a result of his experience, he went to the Olympics with a *goal* and a *belief*, a combination that allowed him to walk away with a silver medal.

Competitive Simulation

In simulation training, you essentially reproduce in training the circumstances, skills, and programs required in competition. It can improve both consistency of performance and consistency of self-belief going into the competition. Simulation, along with extensive repetition of essential competition skills, has served China well in many sports in which the Chinese lead the world today: the traditional martial arts, table tennis, badminton, volleyball, gymnastics, and diving.

When I was teaching a sport psychology course in China, I observed Chinese gymnasts warming up as they do in competition and then going through complete competitive routines for entire training sessions, day after day. Then when these athletes get to a competition, they *know* they can do the routines. Japanese athletes also do extensive simulation training in sports like gymnastics and the martial arts. This kind of training is a major factor enhancing their confidence in their ability to perform flawless routines anytime, anywhere.

Mr. Su, a former member of China's national table tennis team who coached Canada's national team for several years, notes that a high-performance Chinese player will sometimes serve 1,000 balls in a single training session, three times a week. He feels that repetition of certain competitive skills "may be dull" but "necessary." One of the Chinese players told me that the extensive repetition helped him to get the fine feel and fine control of the serve. The same approach is followed for receiving shots—long, short, smashes, and so on.

Another preparation strategy Chinese players use is to put two ping-pong tables together, side by side. The Chinese essentially play on a table that is double the width of a regulation table. The coach or training partner plays the ball from corner to corner so the athlete really has to move to get it. Athletes sometimes play on this double table for 2 full months. After this training, one of the players told me that when he moved back to a regulation table, he felt "much lighter and faster" and the corners seemed "close and easy to get to." This kind of "oversimulation" training helps athletes to have confidence in their ability to get to almost any ball on a regulation-sized table.

In order to develop competition skills and confidence in virtually all sports, it is important to set up some training sessions in which you run through exactly what you must do in the competition. A certain amount of repetition is required to perfect any sport skill, but the quality of that repetition is also extremely important. In preparing for the 1984 Olympic Games, Olympic gold medalist

Sylvie Bernier did nowhere near as many dives off the boards as her Chinese counterparts. However, the dives she did execute were done with the highest quality of effort. She also did much more "mental diving" than her competitors. The quality of effort and mental preparation brought to training is a critical prerequisite for excellence.

To familiarize themselves with a race course, Polish cyclists have used a simulation strategy that involved filming the actual competition course from a bicycle. The athletes then pedalled on a stationary bicycle while watching the film of the competition course unfold. The work load on the bicycle was adapted to meet conditions being viewed on the film, for example, increased resistance for hills.

You must establish a pattern of quality in executing your physical and psychological skills, which means you need to practice doing them well. When focusing on the quality of movement, you would be better off resting if performance skills are starting to deteriorate, rather than pushing on and becoming practiced at subpar-level performance. However, in some sports you also must be able to perform when extremely fatigued. When you are working to increase your capacity to perform well at the end of a long contest, there is value in simulating those fatigued conditions in training so that you are prepared both physically and psychologically and know you can perform under them.

Overtraining Caution

The Chinese philosophy for developing high-performance athletes has the distinct ring that more is better. The more you train, work, and repeat, the better you will be. This holds true in many sports but only to a point. For example, while in China I spoke with a swimming coach visiting from Australia, Forbes Carlile. It concerned him that the Chinese swimmers worked so long and hard that they did not have time to recover physiologically. Their performance was declining rather than improving, which initially made them think that they needed to work even harder.

When engaging in high-intensity training, you always have to be on guard against overtraining, which results in a downward spiral of performance. Overtraining seems to be prevalent during the Olympic year, especially in high-intensity sports. Feeling extremely fatigued even before you get to the workout probably means that your body needs rest more than anything else. Pushing under these conditions is not physiologically sound and also increases the risk of injury. It is a good idea to have some sort of physiological monitoring system to avoid overtraining and injury.

Consistent Thoughts and Focus

To have consistent results you need to have consistently constructive thoughts and focuses going into competitions. If the basic challenge is the same, and your preevent physical preparation, beliefs, and competition focus are basically the same, then your performance should be consistent.

The path to consistency is ultimately cleared by developing a precompetition plan and competition focus plan that you follow systematically. An effective refocusing plan is also required for consistent performance, just in case external hassles begin to interfere with your preplanned constructive thinking. Once you begin to implement these plans systematically, your performance will become more consistent. This in turn will help you to enter a positive spiral: The more consistent performance will enhance your self-confidence, which will then make your performance even more consistent, further raising your confidence.

If we look at the mental pattern of one of Canada's all-time best performers in alpine skiing, we see that there is consistency within her thinking and focus for her best performances, and her worst, but inconsistency of thinking and focus between her best and worst. *Before* her all-time best performances (usually on demanding courses), her activation level was very high; there was an underlying belief in her capacity to win ("I am as capable as many others of winning.") and a personal commitment to be the best she could be. ("Do the best you can.") *During* her best races, on the way down, there was an underlying commitment to speed and to complete concentration on sections of the course being skied or about to be skied.

Before and during her worst competitive performances, which usually occurred on less-demanding courses, her activation level was lower ("not as physically charged"), and her focus was underlined by a lack of confidence ("perhaps not confident enough," "course may be too easy," "wanting to just finish"). This change in mental perspective for the easy courses, or 'flats," interfered with her consistent high-level performance.

In cases where her performance changed significantly from one week to the next, it seemed that her mental framework changed, probably as a result of the different challenge presented by the conditions. For example, if the course had more flats or was not a challenging course, her prerace belief in her ability to rise to the lesser challenge was a bit different, and thereby likely affected her performance.

The few times she skied flat sections really well within a race, her determination and activation levels were up. For example, she skied exceptionally well in a race with long flats when she "had to" in order to be the first overall for the World Cup title. She won the bottom section of the course (flats) in a *very* important race in which she *"really wanted to do well."* She also performed extremely well in another race where the beginning of the race was flat. To perform consistently well, she needed to be highly activated and determined to do well in the flats, or on less challenging courses. Her general pattern on this type of course had been to be less activated and less determined than normal.

For simpler tasks, we know that a higher activation level is often needed to generate a peak performance. Flats were a relatively simple task for this skier. Perhaps she was right when she said, "Maybe I have to work harder because it is easier." On easy courses or flats her concentration may not have been as naturally riveted to sections of the course because she did not always have to be focused to meet the challenge. The course, or at least its flat section, did not *demand* it from her.

It seemed clear that her consistency in good performances would improve if she could enter those courses with more determination, more commitment, higher activation, and more focus on the task. I felt she would gain by having some cues to activate and focus just before entering the flats (or while skiing the flats), to ensure that her body traveled with the most determination and least resistance (e.g., "go after this section," "do it," "tuck," "stay low").

Choosing Your Course

You have the capacity to choose how you feel, think, or focus. Choose to feel positive, not to work against yourself. Refuse to get upset over insignificant things. Choose to give yourself positive reminders before performing. Choose to be as you prefer to be. Focus as you prefer to focus. Perform as you choose to perform. This is something within your capacity, not something magical or beyond reach. You are in control of yourself—mentally and physically.

When attempting to enhance confidence or accept a new and more accurate image of your abilities and overall worth, you can write out or tape reality-based reminders of your ability (See Appendix B for specific examples). You can then think them, read them, or listen to them in a relaxed state away from the competitive setting or on-site before the competition.

When trying to convince or remind yourself of what you *can do*, you should say these things, think them, or imagine them with conviction, with *emotion*, with *force*, even though you may not at first fully believe what you are saying. One of the reasons that negative thoughts (I can't, I'm not that good) are so effective is that you think them with emotion. You don't just say, "I'm no good, I'm going to blow this," in a detached way. You feel it in your gut. So when you say, "I'm ready," "I can do this," you shouldn't say it in a detached way either. You want to say it emphatically, with conviction, and to feel it in your gut.

Olympic high jumper Brigitte Bittner comments, "It is very much like learning a new skill or unlearning a bad habit. You have to repeat it over and over again to erase negative thoughts, which may have been there for a while. It takes time, but eventually the new skill becomes habit."

Building Team Harmony

Harmony among athletes, among coaches, and between athletes and coaches affects almost everything else. Motivation for training, openness to learning, commitment to improved performance, levels of anxiety, feelings of personal acceptance, and overall satisfaction rise and fall with the quality of interpersonal relationships.

When consulting with athletes and coaches, I find that the first concern to be discussed is almost always psychological preparation for competition. However, once we have focused some attention on resolving this issue, a second concern surfaces, and that is team harmony. I often have the feeling that this is the more critical issue because it is one that confronts coaches and athletes almost daily: in training, outside training, while traveling, and in competitive situations. This issue is probably raised second, rather than first, only because it carries a more personal threat.

Team harmony is a realistic goal if you have a commitment to that goal and a *plan* to get there. First you need a mutual commitment to develop or improve interpersonal harmony. Once you have the commitment, you can begin working on your plan.

Small Group Harmony

Some of the most skilled athletes with whom I have worked have had a low tolerance for people. Their tolerance for high-intensity training and for pushing themselves is extremely high. However, when it comes to accepting faults or perceived faults in other people, their tolerance is often lower. When asked about personal strengths and weaknesses, a multiple Olympic medalist responded that her strength was "determination" and her weakness "intolerance of others." My immediate thought was of adding strength to weakness, becoming more determined to be tolerant of others.

During the Olympic year, athletes are incredibly committed to their goal, particularly those who dream of a medal. The stress level and training intensity are noticeably elevated, from the very beginning of the first training camp. As one aspiring Olympian expressed it, "Everyone is out to make the team, so it is pretty hard to be sincerely friendly. It is mostly a surface friendship with the shining knife held behind your back."

Probably because the stress level is up, people complain more and are quicker to overreact to what others are doing. In most cases athletes at all levels would serve themselves better by attempting to be a little more tolerant of events or people who are beyond their immediate control. It takes an incredible amount of energy to devote yourself fully to training for the Olympics or any other important competition. At the end of a hard day, you don't have a lot of mental energy left to get caught up in unproductive hassles—not if you want to have your best shot at your goal. So you need a little plan to avoid unnecessary hassles and to keep people's faults in perspective. You can't control their actions, so don't take responsibility for their faults.

It may be possible to achieve a very challenging goal when facing interpersonal conflicts, but it seems to me that the process of getting there will be much more enjoyable—and the probability of getting there much higher—if you can direct your energies to helping each other progress toward the goal. Destructive bickering and complaining really don't help anyone achieve goals. But, sharing concerns and ideas might.

Promoting Harmony in Training

We have had our fair share of harmony problems on some of the teams with which I have worked. Part of the reason for this is that we had a collection of distinctly different individuals, all of whom were determined and highly committed competitors. Take the case of canoeing. In order to make the national team, athletes compete against each other in individual and in pairs events. Then four competing individuals or two sets of competing pairs are often required to form a team boat comprised of four paddlers. The coaches hope that these four athletes will be cooperative and helpful, or at least tolerant of one another.

Often that is a problem. In one case, disharmony had reached the point that some athletes felt that their teammates hoped that they would not perform well, even after the team had been selected. For example, the team who qualified to compete in the pairs event felt that the pair who did not qualify for that event held resentful feelings and hoped the qualifiers would not do well. It might not have been so bad except that these four people continued to train together, travel together, and compete together for a crew race involving all of them.

In an attempt to resolve some of these problems, I met with that crew and the coach at the first training camp for the Olympic year. I wanted to accomplish three things at that meeting:

1. To get a commitment to a common performance goal
2. To get a commitment to a goal of improved interpersonal harmony
3. To discuss strategies for improving team harmony

The common goal for this group was the best performance possible for each person, which in turn would result in the best performance for the team boat. One by one, each person was asked, and expressed, her specific performance goals for this event, as well as her interpersonal goals. The interpersonal goals that the athletes said they would like to move towards included unity, harmony within the boat, helping each other achieve goals, supporting each other, wanting others to do well, and training together keeping in mind *everyone's* collective goal, which was to be the best they could be.

Some misunderstandings were voiced at this meeting. For example, one athlete expressed her reason for continuing to compete hard against the best pair throughout the season even after the best pair was selected for the team. She wanted to show them that she and her partner were good enough to be in the K-4 (team boat) with them. They wanted to prove themselves, to prove they were not bad, that they were not that far away." As she expressed it, her intent was "to prove myself worthy of a greater commitment from the other pair to the team boat." Unfortunately, this constant competition on the water and during training sessions was not perceived as positive. It was seen as sour grapes, resentment, or animosity directed toward the other pair. It had never been discussed until that moment.

With respect to improving harmony, I attempted to make the following points:

- The more open you can be with each other, the better are your chances of getting along and achieving your goals.
- The most important thing you can do to increase harmony is to make a commitment to do so.
- You must try to express your feelings.
- You must try to give and receive criticism constructively.

I suggested that as a part of every training session, the last 5 minutes be devoted to team members' expressing views or feelings about the workout and about each other. I felt that this was the only way for them to get the best out of each other and the most out of every training session. To achieve high-level performance goals in an Olympic year, which this crew eventually did by winning an Olympic medal, nothing less would be enough.

The after-training reflections revolved around 4 basic questions:

1. What went well?
2. What needs work?
3. What would you like more of from your coach, fellow athletes, or self?
4. What would you like less of from your coach, fellow athletes, or self?

Each person, including the coach, had an opportunity to express herself after each training session: "This went well; that still needs work." "I would appreciate more of this from this person; I would appreciate less of that from that person." Every person did not comment on every area; however, the opportunity to express major feelings on any issue was encouraged by having a preset time to do it every day.

If something one partner was doing was negatively affecting the concentration of another, this time provided a good opportunity to bring up the concern. The best chance for the team to reach its collective goal was provided by discussing and correcting these concerns before they became big problems. We made this task easier by including it as a part of the training session and by encouraging it. As a result, problem-solving discussions were much more likely to occur.

Athletes were reminded that when a criticism is voiced in this context, it is the job of the person offering it to try to phrase it constructively, and it is the job of those on the receiving end to try to receive it in a constructive manner. When receiving criticism, the most important self-imposed question should be, What is his/her *intent*? When giving criticism, it is probably most important to state your intent before you offer the criticism. For example, "I offer this comment because I feel it is important to our goal"; or because "I believe it is the best way to reach the training intensity needed to achieve our goal"; or because "I think it will help our harmony in the long run."

We found that daily discussions at the end of training provided a good opportunity for athletes to practice sharing well-intended, constructively phrased criticism with fellow athletes and the coach, and for coaches and athletes to practice receiving criticism in a constructive way. If there was fairly consistent feedback from a number of people, it was usually a good indication that the criticism was valid and that some action was warranted.

It is equally important to express positive feelings—that something really went well, this felt good, I liked it when you did that, I'd benefit from more of that. Positive statements make you feel good, reinforce that you are on track, motivate you, and build bonds between people.

It is also important to recognize that some of your constructive criticism may not be acted upon. Some team members may disagree. Others may not be able to change or may not want to change a behavior that you would prefer less of. But some of your comments will be acted upon, some will be debated, some will be reflected upon, and ultimately everyone will do better and feel better as a result.

The process I have outlined for posttraining reflections avoids the problem of having to leave a training session harboring resentment toward another person. It allows for the expression of previously unexpressed feelings (e.g., I'm worried that we did not do enough of the right things today to move realistically towards our goal). It enables you to leave a training session having done a brief personal evaluation, having expressed an opinion, and feeling more mentally prepared to come to the next training session with a commitment to get the most out of it. It leads to greater understanding, more valuable training, more enjoyment, more goal-directedness and more support. That is the way to get the most out of everyone.

With small groups of two to six persons this process works well, and everyone can briefly express what's on his or her mind in a short period of time. For larger groups, or teams, perhaps athletes can be broken down into smaller meaningful units that promote interaction.

Athletes' Suggestions for Harmony

Six months before the 1984 Olympic Games, Alwyn Morris (1984 Olympic gold medalist) expressed this feeling: "Harmony is by far the most important aspect in my mind for coping this year. Feeling that you are for everyone and everyone is for you, without feeling jealous, would be an enormous experience, especially having it happen at the Olympics."

How might we accomplish this? The question I posed to the athletes was, "What do you think you could do, or the team could do, to increase harmony this year?"

Their suggestions included the following:

- I think that if we all just make a little more effort to get along with everyone else, things will run much more smoothly.
- Each team member can help him- or herself by learning to tolerate others better. You can't always expect others to help you—so help yourself by tolerating others.
- Everybody may need to give a little to ensure that everybody pulls in the same direction—toward gold medals.

- Accept team members as they are—their habits, their flaws, their personality quirks, and their way of living—and try to work together as a whole team.
- Avoid backbiting and gossiping about teammates. If you don't like something that someone does, don't tell everyone; that just leads to more people getting mad at that person for no reason.
- Care a little more about your neighbor. Spend some positive time with one another.
- Introduce some fun things and enjoyable team activities to reduce the tension between athletes.
- Stop the practice of "ranking" athletes and basing treatment on that—we understand priorities, but we are all people.
- If any "beefs" with coaches or managers or athletes arise, have a talk—one to one.
- Discuss problems openly with all parties present.
- Discuss solutions and implement them.

Communication and Mind Reading

Not everything that is faced can be changed but nothing can be changed until it is faced.

James Baldwin

G ood communication skills are among the most important ingredients contributing to performance enhancement and life satisfaction. One of the biggest problems in communication is that we often expect other people to be mind readers. We expect them to understand our feelings without our ever expressing them. We expect loved ones to understand our feelings from a simple gesture or an unspoken thought, and are disappointed when they don't. Why doesn't he understand *my* feelings, *my* perspective? Why doesn't she respond to my needs? Why doesn't he know when I need a hug?

Mind Reading

It is difficult to understand another person's feelings or appreciate another's perspective if it is never expressed clearly. It is difficult, if not impossible, for someone to respond to another person's needs when he or she does not know what those needs are. If you express your feelings and/or perceived needs, there is at least the possibility of someone understanding and responding. At least they are made aware of your feelings and therefore have the possibility of acting.

You have three choices: (a) you can choose not to express your feelings and continue to be misunderstood and/or mistreated; (b) you can work on improving your mind-reading abilities (transmitting and receiving thoughts directly with no talk); or (c) you can begin to express your feelings. It seems to me that the third option, difficult as it may sometimes be, is the most realistic choice in terms of improving relationships and reaping all the other benefits that follow.

One reason people do not express feelings is the fear that they will be rejected for saying what they feel—that their self-worth or overall acceptability is on the line. The problem with not expressing feelings is that it allows problems to grow without addressing solutions. It is so much easier and more beneficial to express real feelings when problems are small and manageable rather than to wait until they are *big* and unmanageable. Take, for example, a relationship you have that begins with a few small problems. No big deal. All relationships have some problems. However, if they are never openly expressed or discussed, the problem is often reluctantly "accepted" with resentment. The feelings smoulder internally and no mutual solutions are sought. Over time, more and more problems surface; little things "bug" you, but remain unspoken, and as a result, unsolved. Finally you reach the point where you must talk or leave. So you decide to talk. The person across from you asks in a surprised tone, "What is it that's bothering you?" You pull out a list of 100 things that bug you, which you have collected over the year(s). The little problem is now *big*. By this time so much resentment has often built up that it is extremely difficult or even too late to work out harmonious solutions.

It is not easy to express real feelings, especially when they are not highly flattering, when you feel hurt, sad, or rejected because of something someone has done, or when you feel that you have been treated unfairly or inconsiderately. It may be difficult to express these feelings when they first surface, but in the long run it is much more difficult for you and for others if you do not express them. Problems are prevented and problems are solved by expressing feelings on a continuous basis.

Expressing a feeling does not necessarily imply anything about a solution to the problem. You simply communicate, "This is how I feel (e.g., rejected, abandoned, empty) about what you did." You may not have a solution (yet), but you have a feeling and you are sharing it. By expressing your feelings, you have spared the other person from relying on mind-reading.

In most cases, sharing the feeling will eventually result in some sort of solution. At least some options will be identified for consideration. If a person listens (even a little), it will lead to more understanding than previously existed. Making the other person aware of your feelings is as important as the specific solution because a basic understanding of how you are feeling may allow that person to move beyond a specific solution to avoid a host of other problems.

Communication Skills

The ability to express feelings, to communicate clearly, and to constructively criticize is not easily acquired. It is a life-long process of learning and worthy of a good deal of effort because it affects every relationship we will ever have, inside or outside of sport. The communication skills of refined listening, clear speaking, and staying expressive need to be developed and refined over time.

Refined Listening

This is probably the most important and yet least developed communication skill. Listening involves your ears, your eyes, and your heart. What is this person *really* saying, what is she really feeling? It is not always written on the surface. If you are not sure how someone is feeling about a decision or a performance, you may have to ask, "How are you *really feeling* about this in your gut?" Becoming a keen observer also allows you to listen better.

To listen well, you should forget about how *you* see the situation and focus fully on how *the other person* sees it. Don't interrupt; don't judge. Let the other person express feelings while you focus on listening and understanding. Eliminate the "yeah but's." Avoid challenging him or her. Don't point fingers. Just listen and feel that person's perspective. Soak in it before responding.

Clear Speaking

When you do respond, be sure that you express yourself clearly. When your coach gives you instructions, how clear is the message? On more than one occasion I have heard coaches ask athletes to "concentrate more." What does that mean? How are you translating that into action? What are you supposed to do?

I have asked athletes what they do when the coach says, "Concentrate more." Interestingly enough, many try to *look* like they are concentrating more with a serious expression and a wrinkled forehead. Many do not have a clear understanding of what is being asked. It is best for a coach to say *exactly* what he or she wants (e.g., "be more explosive on the take-off, plant sooner, focus on staying in synch with your partner"). If you are not getting this exact feedback, ask your coach to be more explicit so that what *you* think the coach is saying and what the coach thinks he or she is saying are one and the same when translated into action. Can you encourage your coach to give you clarification when the message is not crystal-clear? Can you also attempt to express your messages and suggestions as clearly as possible? Athletes too are often unclear in their verbal messages.

Staying Expressive

For a team to perform to potential and for athletes not to interfere with each other's psychological preparation in important events, something will be gained by open discussion with one another in advance of the competition. Such discussion is particularly important in team events. It is best that each member of an interdependent unit such as in paddling crews, pairs skaters, and hockey lines, know the precompetition needs and preparation idiosyncrasies of the others. Preevent worries about what teammates are doing, or conflict between members of the same unit just before the start of the race or game can easily result in a very strong team having a substantially lower performance. Do not let your teammates' varied ways of preparing affect your preparation and performance. What is best for them on-site is not necessarily what is best for you; doing what is best for each will allow the best team performance.

Jack Donohue and Cal Botterill both feel that staying expressive *within* the game is very important in a team sport like basketball. That means talking to each other and encouraging each other on-court while playing the game. Calling out plays, giving each other verbal and physical support, and being genuinely positive on court (e.g., "good play," "way to go," "we're in control," a slap on the hands, pat on the back,) can help a team to achieve its goal. If staying expressive is important for your team, a team meeting could be held to clarify what is meant by staying expressive, to set some expectations for it to happen, to encourage each other to indicate when it does happen, to rehearse it in practice and to do it in games.

Giving Criticism Constructively

There is immense value in explaining the intent of your criticism *before* giving it. Good examples are "I'm telling you this in hopes of improving our relationship"; "I want to help improve the consistency of your skilled performance"; "I need to get something off my chest that has been bothering me"; "My intent is to help and not to hurt, regardless of how it might come out." Explaining your intent *first* is probably the single most important thing you can do when giving criticism.

Deciding to state your intent before you state your criticism will force you to think about your own purpose. This in turn should help you phrase the criticism appropriately. In addition, if you can think about how the criticized person is likely to react, it may also help you to phrase the criticism more constructively. Phrasing a criticism constructively includes expressing your intent and delivering your message in a clear, open, and concerned way. In constructive commmunication there is never a desire to put the other person down or buoy yourself up, as often exists in power or status games. A person delivering criticism has the most to gain if he or she can express it as constructively as possible.

Receiving Criticism Constructively

A person receiving criticism has the most to gain if he can receive it as constructively as possible. However, many athletes and coaches are not that good at receiving criticism. They often interpret criticism as a personal attack, a put-down, rejection, or lack of appreciation for all of their good qualities. When *you* are being criticized, the anger or irritation that surfaces in your gut may result from a misperception or misunderstanding of another's intent. It is true that someone is pointing out what they perceive as an imperfection, and that may pierce your ideal image of yourself. Someone is telling you that, in this instance, they did not see you as perfect or as compatible as you would like to be (or have them think you are). But why are they telling you this?

When criticism comes from a person who cares about you and your performance, the intent of that criticism is usually constructive or helpful, regardless of how it might be delivered. The criticism is usually aimed at resolving a perceived problem, correcting a performance error, or improving a relationship. The hope is to make you and/or a relationship better. Listen to criticism in this light. Learn from it instead of putting up protective barriers, and you will have a much better opportunity to grow from it, personally, interpersonally, and performance-wise.

You might want to develop a little plan of action to do this. The next time criticism is fired your way, try to momentarily suspend your emotional reaction (or overreaction). Put it on hold; "tree it" temporarily. Step outside yourself—outside your protective shield. **Listen** to what the person is saying. Ask yourself the following questions:

- What is this person's intent?
- Can I gain anything from this input (e.g., understanding myself, my performance, or the other person)?
- Is the criticism serving the needs of the person giving it as a tension outlet or as a means of giving a sense of personal control?
- Can it help me understand him or her?
- Can it help me grow (is it directed towards my improvement)?
- Can it help our relationship?
- Is there anything here I can act upon to come closer to my goals (personal, interpersonal, or performance)?

Plan how you will use the information being communicated. Let's say your coach has given you some performance criticism that you feel is largely accurate. To get the best or most out of him (a) tell him you agree with the criticism or with certain parts of it; (b) repeat back the contents of his criticism in your own words to make sure that you have understood him correctly; (c) ask him for precise suggestions regarding how you might best act on the criticism; (d) commit yourself to act on the criticism and develop a plan of action; and (e) if you disagree with parts of his criticism, or with the manner in which it was communicated, clearly express your disagreement and your reasons for it.

In case performance feedback still occasionally comes through in a less constructive fashion, especially at the competition site, you should have your own plan to translate it into positive action. For example, "stop, breathe out, relax." Translate the message into what *you have to do* to set up properly for that skill or obstacle. Take on that responsibility yourself. Run the correct image through your head several times. "Feel it" going well. Then set it aside. It should unfold as you imagined because you have focused on *what to do* and secured that message in your head through your repeated imagery. When the time comes to begin setting up for the challenge within the competition, you should be able to act upon that successful image automatically. For some athletes a setup cue just before executing the skill may also be helpful.

The more proficient you become at self-direction and self-criticism, the less you need to rely on the criticism of others. But at times, direct, honest, and objective criticism from another person can give you a perspective for improvement that you may not see in yourself. Improving your communication skills is a lifelong process. Like other skills it requires a plan practice, reflections, and refinement. You will do yourself and your loved ones a favor by beginning that process now.

Relaxation and Imagery

I n this chapter I will make specific comments about the use of relaxation and mental imagery for competitive preparation. I don't intend to present basic relaxation and imagery procedures in great detail, as these topics have already been addressed in *In Pursuit of Excellence* (1980) and in other sport psychology books. My comments are related more to applying these procedures effectively in the real situation.

Butterflies in Formation

Sport psychologist Madeleine Hallé has done some interesting work on the psychological preparation of gymnasts. If an athlete is experiencing preevent anxiety or fear, she suggests that the acceptance of that feeling be part of the coping strategy. For example, if a gymnast is afraid of doing a move in training, a recommended self-talk would go something like this: "I know I'm afraid of the move (accept), but it's important to me. I need the move and I want to do it (cope)." Likewise, if an athlete is feeling nervous before an event, instead of just saying, "Stop, focus on the task," her or his initial response would be acceptance of the feeling. "I accept the fact that I'm excited or nervous and it's normal." Then the focus would shift to some cue for strengthening a feeling of being ready or for refocusing on the task ahead.

When it actually comes time to compete, and you step out onto the floor in an important event, you would have to be made of stone not to feel something in your gut—butterflies or a rush of adrenaline. Under such circumstances telling yourself to relax or shifting your focus to relaxation is not likely to make you feel relaxed. The most you can expect from it is to slightly reduce the tension. The tension you continue to feel, even if you shift to "relax," is normal and should be viewed as such. If you view it otherwise, you may start to worry that the relaxation strategy is not working and become even more tense.

The important thing to remember is that being nervous will not negatively affect your performance as long as you can direct your focus to what you must *do* to perform. If you shift your focus away from results toward performing the task immediately at hand, the butterflies may even help. As Coach Donohue so aptly expresses it, "It's not a question of getting rid of the butterflies, it's a question of getting them to fly in formation." If your focus is in the right place—for example, on reminding yourself of your best task focus and then on riveting your attention to that task—the butterflies *will* fly in formation.

Relaxation

For many athletes, relaxation has not been an effective strategy for dealing with the stress of competition, especially if used to the exclusion of other stress management strategies. It is very difficult to get a real relaxation effect by focusing directly on relaxation in the face of stress. Relaxing as you stretch out in the silence and comfort of your own home or gym is light-years away from relaxing as you step out onto the floor for an important competition. Relaxation on-site in the heat of competition, or when confronted with high levels of stress, does not come easily. It requires practice during training sessions, before and during competitions, and in everyday stressful situations. You must move beyond relaxing under nonstressful conditions to relaxing under progressively more stressful conditions. If you fail to take this step, the relaxation approach will be virtually useless as a means of immediate precompetition activation control. If you become anxious before the start of your event, it is often better to remind yourself of your readiness and your best event focus than to focus on relaxation.

For those of you who are just beginning to develop basic relaxation skills, cassette tapes are a good idea. Several have been designed to help athletes with relaxation and mental imagery. The best commerically available tapes that I know of are those created by Swedish sport psychologist Lars-Eric Unestahl. His program consists of three audio cassettes, entitled Mental Training I, II, and III.[1]

The most commonly used procedure for teaching basic relaxation is progressive muscle relaxation. In this procedure, you first tense a muscle group and then relax it. The tension-relaxation process was developed to help "normal," untrained people learn where their muscles are so that they would know where to send relaxation signals, as well as to help them distinguish between tension and relaxation. As an athlete, you already know where your muscles are, and you know the feelings of muscular tension and relaxation. As a result you are probably better connected to your body than any other group of people.

Most athletes with whom I have worked prefer not to bring on muscle tension when their goal is relaxation. I recommend skipping the tension and going directly to the relaxation. In a nonstressful setting it is not difficult for most athletes to bring on a relaxation response within a few minutes by sitting or lying down quietly and thinking themselves into a relaxed state. Let the relaxation spread through your body as you exhale slowly. You can attain deep and restful relaxation in this way for recovery from fatigue, for self-suggestions, for relaxation breaks, for presleep imagery, or for going to sleep.

For relaxation to become your natural response to stresses in the environment, you must use every opportunity to practice it. One-breath relaxation is one of the most useful procedures for employment in the real situation (on-site). Take a deep breath (long, slow inhalation), followed by a long, slow exhalation. Try it now. Couple the exhalation with the thought "relax" and let your body relax. Do it several times in a row. Practice one-breath relaxation before exams, at border crossings (anything to declare?), in interviews,

---

[1]For more information on these tapes, write Mouvement Publications, 109 East State Street, Ithaca, New York, 14850 USA or to VEJE, Box 16017, S-700 16 Orebro, Sweden.

in the dentist's chair, in arguments, when someone cuts you off on the road, and in simulated and real sport competitions. You will then be practiced at using the strategy and will be more capable of using it when you need it most.

For sport-specific relaxation it is a good idea to *practice* relaxing specific muscles while you are actively engaged in your sport. This should include focusing on relaxing muscles that do not need to be tense (a) while in the "ready" or "start" position, as well as (b) while executing the actual movement skills. For example, while running, paddling, or cycling, relax your "jaw," "hands," "grip," "shoulders," "arms," "back," "breathing," and if your sport skill has a recovery phase, think "relax" on the recovery.

Mental Imagery

The very best athletes have developed an excellent capacity for clear, vivid imagery and use it extensively. If you can develop and refine your imagery, it can serve a variety of useful purposes:

- *To see success*. Many of the best athletes "see" themselves achieving their goals on a regular basis—both performing the skills at a high level and seeing the desired performance outcome.
- *To motivate*. Before or during training sessions, calling up images of your goals for that session, or of a past or future competition or competitor can serve a motivational purpose. It can vividly remind you of your objective, which can result in increased intensity in training.
- *To perfect skills*. Mental imagery is often used to facilitate the learning and refinement of skills or skill sequences. The best athletes "see" and "feel" themselves performing perfect skills, programs, routines, or plays on a very regular basis.
- *To familiarize*. Mental imagery can be effectively used to familiarize yourself with all kinds of things, such as a competition site, a race course, a complex play pattern or routine, a precompetition plan, an event focus plan, a media interview plan, a refocusing plan, or the strategy you plan to follow.
- *To set the stage for performance*. Mental imagery is often an integral part of the precompetition plan, which helps set the mental stage for a good performance. The best athletes often do a

complete mental run-through of the key elements of their performance. This helps draw out their desired precompetition feelings and focus. It also helps keep negative thoughts from interfering with a positive pregame focus.

* *To refocus.* Mental imagery can be useful in helping you to refocus when the need arises. For example, if a warm-up is feeling sluggish, imagery of a previous best performance or previous best event focus can help get things back on track. You can also use imagery as a means of refocusing within the event, by imagining what you should focus on and feeling that focus.

Most of the best athletes call up images of performance skills from the inside, as if they were inside their own bodies actually doing it, but that is not true for all of them. Some visualize in a mixed fashion, alternating "inside" and "outside" views, but always "feeling" as they view.

In well-developed imagery you do not merely see the image, you experience a feeling or recall an experience through the image. When you create or recall an image in your mind, you should attempt to enter fully into that image with all your senses. See, feel, hear, touch, and do as you do or would like to do in the real situation. Above all else, *feel* what you are doing.

To become highly proficient at the constructive use of imagery, you have to use it every day—on your way to training, during training, after training, and in the evenings before sleeping. The best athletes I have ever met did not follow a specific mental imagery training program. They simply used imagery regularly and kept at it; gradually their images became clear and controlled, much as if they had been artists learning to draw. In a way, imagery *is* like drawing: you create images with your brain, you draw from your inner feelings. In order to improve the clarity of the image and the ease with which you can call up an image or feeling, you need to keep at it. You need to do it *every day*. Set a goal to do that.

If you want to perfect and use mental imagery to your fullest advantage, you can start by doing two things. In every training session, before you execute any skill or combination of skills, *first* do it in imagery as perfectly and precisely as possible. See, feel, or experience yourself moving through the actions in your mind as you would like them actually to unfold. In competitions, before the event starts, mentally recall the event focus plan, significant plays, skills, movements, reactions, or feelings that you want to carry into the event.

If you are wondering how much you need to practice mental imagery, I can't give you a precise answer, any more than I can tell you how many times you need to practice doing a handstand before you perfect it. I can only say that you have to keep at it until you get it, until your imagery is clear, fluid, easy to call up, and within your control. It will definitely improve with practice.

In a sport like alpine skiing, good imagery control is very important because it helps athletes learn the course more thoroughly and more quickly. That there is an element of risk when pushing limits (riding the fine line) makes knowing the course all the more important. Therefore, imagery in alpine skiing has the unique function of risk reduction, confidence building, and freeing the athlete to really "go after" the performance. Many athletes in this sport have told me that drawing a sketch of the course is a valuable addition to their imagery in terms of learning the course.

If you can "see" and "feel" yourself perform flawlessly in imagery, it can also remind you of your potential and can leave you with a positive feeling about how you will perform. In less than ideal circumstances, such as arriving late or having a not-so-hot warm-up, good imagery may also help you to refocus on the positive.

The leading skiers on the women's national alpine ski team had the best-developed imagery that I had encountered with any group. They had clearer imagery, used it more extensively, had better control over it, and experienced it almost exclusively from the inside. They could clearly visualize the course and ski it "from the inside" as if they were inside themselves, inside their own bodies, going down the slope. Lars-Eric Unestahl also found that the best Swedish skiers had superior mental imagery skills. They could ski the course in imagery closer to the actual time it took and were also better able to experience the course through imagery. It is interesting to note that from the time a race course is inspected to the time of the actual race, it is not uncommon for the top skiers to ski that course, or sections of it, 50 times *in imagery*.

Only one member of the Canadian national ski team had poorly developed imagery skills. The general control of her images (4 out of a perfect 10) and clarity of images (4 out of 10) needed improvement if imagery was to be a valuable technique for her to use. Up to this point she had been attempting to use imagery at races but had not been doing it in training. It is probably unrealistic to think you can perfect a skill in competition when you never practice it at any other time.

If she was going to use imagery to her full advantage, she would have to practice it more. She had to learn to control or successfully correct unwanted images (e.g., images of "crashing" or "jumping like a kangaroo" or "snowplowing"). A negative image may pop into your head now and then, but you don't want to have that image take over or become the final one left in your mind before a performance. With practice you can improve control of imagery.

I suggested that she set a goal to do some imagery every day for the next few months if she really wanted to improve her ability to control her images. I asked her to consider some of the following exercises, which you can adapt for your sport or your needs.

- Every day during training, try to visualize the course and then feel yourself skiing the course or sections of it.
- On the way up the lift, in training, imagine yourself skiing a section of the course as you would like to in competition.
- Three evenings a week before going to sleep, try to feel yourself skiing the course (or section) as you would like. If a problem arises (e.g., negative image), *stop* the image and go back up the hill, above the problem. Then continue down the hill, correcting the problem.
- Off-season, or away from training when relaxing, look at various images around you, close your eyes and try to "see" them clearly.
- "See" and "feel" yourself doing other activities in imagery (e.g., paddling, bicycling, or running).
- Try to recall the good feelings you have had before and after some of your best performances.

I told this skier that it might take a few weeks of imagery work before she would notice the improvement in the clarity and feeling of her images and in her ability to control or correct unwanted images. But it would happen with practice. As her imagery improved, it was of much more value to her in preparation for race situations. She used imagery to become more familiar with the course, to be more confident in her ability to ski the course, and to be more consistent in "feeling" herself go down the course perfectly in her mind, before the actual race. Interestingly, one of the first times that she ever experienced clear and controlled imagery of the *whole course* before the race, she had her best-ever race performance. First, she did clear imagery of the course (four gates at a time) all the way down while inspecting the course; then she skied the whole course in imagery as if she were actually inside herself skiing down—with no errors.

Once your imagery becomes good, you can take full advantage of it for a variety of situations. For example, you can use it to "see" yourself behaving in a completely confident way at a competition, gaining full control in a stressful situation, or easily expressing your feelings in an interpersonal situation. You can also help get yourself into your desired prerace feeling state through imagery. One skier, whose imagery is extremely good, was able to "feel good and smooth and get into the glide of it" with her imagery. In her prerace preparation plan, she was able "to take advantage of past good feelings," which "helped a lot with the first three or four gates." She could relax, think back to what felt good, and call up that feeling in imagery during the warm-up.

The mental imagery questions on Table 13.1 were drawn from a questionnaire initially developed by Mahoney and Avener (1977) and revised for skiing by Rotella, Gansneder, Ojala, and Billing (1980). We used some of their questions assessing the skiers' proficiency at visual imagery skills. The averaged responses from the women on the National Alpine ski team are presented in the right-hand column, next to each question. The responses are categorized into (a) team members who won more than one World Cup event and (b) the remainder of the National Team. It is clear from their responses that the better skiers used imagery more extensively, had better control over their images, viewed things from the inside, and had vivid mental images. Their refined imagery skills likely contributed to their refined performance skills.

Table 13.1   Compared Responses of National Ski Team Members to Mental Imagery Questions*

1. To what extent do you use visual imagery (mental pictures) in your training and in preparation for your competition?

   0 1 2 3 4 5 6 7 8 9 10   Average Responses
   Not at all   Very   World Cup event winners   9.5
                    extensively
                                  Remaining members of
                                  National Team   8.5

2. When you are trying to picture something mentally (e.g., skiing in a race), how much difficulty do you have in getting the image to do what you want it to? That is, is it easy or difficult for you to control your mental pictures?

   0 1 2 3 4 5 6 7 8 9 10   World Cup event winners   9.0
   Very   Very
   difficult   easy   Remaining members of
                                  National Team   7.7

3. When you practice something mentally, do you "see" yourself as an external observer would (e.g., from a distance, with your entire body visible like a movie character) or do you "see things as you would normally (i.e., through your eye sockets, with such body parts as your face and neck unseen)? That is, in mental practice, do you try to get inside your body and experience the sensations involved or do you try to get outside your body and view yourself as a coach might?

   0 1 2 3 4 5 6 7 8 9 10   World Cup event winners   0.5
   Exclusively   Equal   Exclusively
   inside   mixture outside   Remaining members of
                                  National Team   2.7

4. How vivid or clear are your mental images?

   0 1 2 3 4 5 6 7 8 9 10   World Cup event winners   9.0
   Very   Very
   unclear   vivid   Remaining members of
                                  National Team   7.4

Note. For an additional mental imagery assessment, which we found useful, see Appendix A.

Video-Images

Videotapes can be quite useful in terms of developing and reinforcing constructive images. Often, videotapes have been used in a negative way. For example, in game films a coach may single out an athlete at a team meeting by rerunning his errors, over and over. In such cases, much of the potential positive value of the video is lost. Self-confidence can be weakened, coach-athlete relations can be hampered, and an athlete may be embarrassed or angered to the point that he or she is unable to focus well on a constructive lesson from the video at hand; and, furthermore, there is also the critical problem of leaving with an error image inside the head.

If your goal is to correct an error, stop the video image at the error and think of specifically what you need to do to correct the error. If the coach is there, she or he can describe in a nonaccusing way what you should do to make that correction. Take a moment to absorb the correction and run it through in your own imagery a few times. The image you want to rerun is the successful image. If you have already executed a skill extremely well, or hope to, rerunning the successful sequence on the video or in your head can be useful.

Preventing Errors

Crookenton (1982) took a group of people and had them hit tennis balls over a net one after another. He found that if the person in front hit the ball *into* the net, the probability of the next person hitting into the net was much higher. It seems to happen in all kinds of things where you can miss, fall, or crash. Falling off a balance beam is a good example. Once one gymnast falls off the balance beam, the probability of others falling off after her is greatly increased.

Olympic high jumper Brigitte Bittner says she "always likes to watch people who I know should be able to make the height. I try not to watch poorer jumpers." When you perform after watching a miss or error, the chances of error seem to increase unless you have a way to ensure that the error image does not "stick" in your mind. One way of overcoming a negative picture is to introduce a positive image and run it through several times. In the same way that negative images can set you up for errors, positive images can help you overcome them.

At one of the first World Cup downhill skiing events during the 1984-85 season, three of our skiers had problems on the same corner. The coach had taken those three skiers to the corner before they raced and had them watch other skiers taking the wrong line on the corner. After watching, one skier said, "I'm not going to do that," but in the heat of the race, she did exactly the same thing when she got to that corner. A problem like this can often be solved if, after watching the error, you focus on the correction. For example, in this case instead of thinking about what you are *not* going to do, think about what you *are* going to do. Then run that correct image in your head three or four times. This should increase your chances of doing it well in the event.

Brian Orser, winner of both the short and long free-skating programs at the 1984 Olympic Games, has made excellent use of positive imagery by drawing upon videotapes and upon the images in his own head. "Going through it mentally is almost like having an extra practice. I visualize the figures and recreate the *feeling* of the turns. I actually go through the motions." Orser had a professional television crew make a videotape that he began using before the Olympics. The tape repeats each clean element of both a short and long program 10 times before moving to the next one and concludes with a complete program, reinforcing "a perfect image" in Brian's mind. "I watch myself do perfect elements 10 times. It creates a very positive feeling." Orser watched that "perfect" image every day for a week before the Olympics. He felt that his imagery helped his elements unfold as cleanly in the competition as they had in his imagination.

For team-sport athletes involved in a play-off series, positive video images may also be useful. For example, where a team has had some excellent games followed by some poorer performances, video images of the earlier best performances could help some players to rebuild confidence and to create a positive image for the remaining game(s). Batting or shooting slumps are also good examples of situations where videos of great or best performances might be helpful.

Some skiers have found it effective to watch videos of the best racers skiing down the competition course for two reasons. First, the skier can see what must be done to set up for a gate or obstacle and can run it in imagery. Second, viewing the tape gets the skier "fired up." They point out that coaches' comments can help *if* they help focus on what has to be done rather than on past mistakes or negative thoughts.

One of our younger skiers on the World Cup circuit had trouble on a difficult corner gate on all four training runs in a downhill course. She was worried about the corner, so she decided to make use of her imagery in an attempt to solve the problem before the race. She sat and looked closely at that corner, deciding how she could best ski it. She then ran the corner in imagery about 20 times in a row. For the first several attempts, she could not ski it correctly in imagery, but with persistence she began to get a controlled and successful image. In the actual race she skied the corner very well for the first time, but only after setting the correct pattern in her mind. The correction focus was effective.

Many of the world's most successful athletes have learned to use relaxation and imagery to their benefit. You, too, can reap benefits of these techniques by systematically practicing imagery and by developing an appropriate, positive focus.

Media Plan

For a major event like the Olympic Games, where the "hype" is at an all-time high, external stressors are intensi-fied. Correspondence, telephone calls, well-wishers, autograph seekers, hangers-on, bureaucracy, crowds, transportation delays, traffic, security, and the media seem to constantly test an athlete's ability to maintain a normal existence. Steve Podborski, three-time Olympian and Canada's first winner of the overall World Cup men's downhill title, commented that the environment at the Games tends to be "very distracting compared to normal." More media coverage, more officials, different application of rules, and transportation problems are only a few of the situations that can potentially overload the athlete. Because of the distractions created by being "hounded" by the media before the 1980 Olympics, Podborski's bottom line in preparing for the 1984 Games was, "It's better to be interviewed after you win than before you lose." Podborski obviously learned from his experiences.

Media contact does not have to be considered a negative factor. It does, however, require careful planning, just as does your performance. Although many of you will never face the same magnitude of media coverage as exists for high-profile athletes at the Olympic Games, most of you will face the press at some point in your career. In this chapter I will share some insights and experiences that may help you develop a protocol for meeting the press while protecting your performance.

In preparing for the media, probably the most important thing a team can do is to establish a media protocol and make sure everyone understands it. Podborski suggests the following protocol for alpine skiing (a high-profile sport):

- *Press Conference.* Hold 5 days prior to the event for general questioning about the village, food, site, transportation, and course. Hold another after the event if necessary.
- *Stand-ups.* Allow interviews in *finish area only* (or equivalent) each day following your performance (e.g., how was your run? etc.).
- *Promos* (Promotional shots). Photos can be filed early and given to media people to use.

Media Protocol

The ground rules that are laid down for communication with the media should reflect what athletes and coaches feel is in the best interest of the team's performance. Podborski suggests that "We tell the press when we're ready; put the onus on them to be ready when the athlete is ready rather than their dictating the schedule." He also points out the "need for a press kit so reporters are prepared and don't waste time with simple, dumb questions" (e.g., How tall are you? How old are you? etc.). If a reporter with no background asks that sort of question, Podborski suggests directing the reporter to the information in the press kit.

If a reporter collars you in the street or outside the finish area, rely on the protocol established. Make it clear that you are responsible to others not to make exceptions. Tell the reporter to attend the stand-up interviews in the finish area or the press conference.

Jayne Torvill and Christopher Dean, the 1984 Olympic gold medalists and four-time world ice-dancing champions, were flooded with interview requests for as much as a month before the 1984 World Championships held in Ottawa (Cleary, 1984). They agreed to do one precompetition interview from the multitude of international media requests. That had become their standard precompetition practice with respect to the media. After each segment of their competition, they briefly met the media as a group again—for example, following the compulsory dance and the original set pattern. They were open to selected personal interviews only *after* their last competition of the championships in free dancing. There were 300 media persons attending the World Figure Skating Championships and 8,200 accredited media persons at the 1984 L.A. Olympics. With such a high level of media interest at these events, obviously some protocol must be established to protect athletes from being overwhelmed or distracted by media requests.

For athletes and coaches, the media are a double-edged sword. On the one hand, you want the media coverage because it gives you and your sport recognition, which can be both satisfying and beneficial. On the other hand, you do not want to let the media interfere with your chances of realizing your dream. As Griffiths (1983) points out, the media can be used productively. "In return for interviews, stories, unique insight, and simple cooperation, the press offers a precious commodity called exposure. Cultivating the press, no matter how painful, will pay big dividends for amateur sport." Then as one of our Olympic coaches queried, "How do we manage the media so we get the coverage and they get the news, yet no conflicts arise?"

Canoeing is a relatively low-profile sport that, like all others, receives unprecedented coverage during the Olympics. We began developing a media plan for canoeing at the first training camp of the Olympic year. At a general team meeting, we discussed the importance of being prepared to deal with the media, and we set some expectations regarding the coverage the team might get. I later met with the coaches and five of the most experienced athletes, whose track records gave them the best shot at Olympic medals. At this meeting one of those athletes, who was preparing for his first Olympics, said, "I didn't think about preparing for the media. I was thinking about my preparation for my race."

As I indicated to them, anyone who has a chance for a medal will be sought out before the event. Anyone who is expected to perform well and either *does* or *does not* will be sought out (and found!) after the event. And if anything unusual or bizarre happens, (e.g., a crash, a broken paddle, an open conflict, an unexpected event), reporters will want to talk with someone. Reporters see that as their job, their reason for being there, and they will do it. Our preparation objective was to avoid letting *their* reason for being there interfere with *our* reason for being there.

Our basic plan was to avoid conflicts whenever possible; and when they were impossible to avoid, to have a plan to minimize their potentially negative effect. The ground rules that were laid down for media communication reflected what the athletes and coaches felt was in the best interest of the team's performance. The first step was to develop a team media availability plan that specifically stated when and where the athletes would be available for interviews. We decided that athletes would be available in the finish area for 10 to 20 minutes *following* their event or training session. The contact person for arranging an interview was specified as the team manager or coach.

The team decided that athletes would not receive calls directly in their living quarters until they were completely finished with their competitions. Calls would be routed through the coach or manager to avoid unwanted distractions. It was also decided that if an athlete felt strongly about not being interviewed until the final was over, his or her wishes would be respected because it was in the best interest of that athlete's mental preparation and performance. In this case, the coach agreed to take on the interviews for that athlete until the competition was over.

The time that athletes felt was most important to be insulated from media people or others was during their final stages of mental preparation, especially the last 30 minutes before the event. It was therefore decided that *no interviews* at the competition site would be given by athletes before their race on a race day. In the area where athletes underwent their final preparation, a coach or manager was available to ward off unwanted intrusions.

We felt it was unnecessary to hold a precompetition press conference because nothing newsworthy had happened yet, and in a low-profile sport something has to happen before press conferences are well attended. Reporters could, however, attend a pre-Olympic Training Camp if they wished to interview athletes or get some background material (e.g., photos, etc.). Additionally, if athletes had some very outstanding results or something newsworthy to share, a press conference could be called after the competition. Table 14.1 depicts the plan devised by the paddlers.

Once we had finalized this basic media availability plan, it was circulated to the media liaison person for the Olympic Association. We then needed a plan to prepare athletes for giving interviews and for being approached "off-limits." In case an athlete was approached in an "off-limits" time or place, each individual had a simple, polite, and firm preplanned reply: "There is a team media policy that I must follow. I can't talk now; see me after the event in the finish area."

Table 14.1   1984 Canadian Olympic Canoe Team Media Availability Plan

---

1. **Reporters** are invited to attend our pre-Olympic training camp in Sacramento, California, for interviews or background materials.

   They must contact:
   Head Coach Frank Garner at the national office (phone number)
   or
   Team Manager Tim Sample at (phone number-home)
   (phone number-office)

2. There will **not** be a precompetition press conference, but if the athlete(s) or team have very outstanding performance(s), a press conference will be called after the competition.

3. **Race day:** *No* interviews at the competition site will be given by athletes before their race on a race day.

4. **Postrace:** Athletes will be available for 10 to 20 minutes *following* their event or training session in the finish area.

   Note: The contact person for arranging interviews is the head coach or team manager.

5. Athletes will not receive phone calls directly. These calls will be directed through the head coach or manager.

6. Coaches and support staff will be available for interviews upon request, through the head coach or manager.

   The Canadian Olympic Canoe Team's main goal is to win medals at the 1984 Olympics in Lake Casitus, California. In order to achieve our objectives, the coaches and athletes believe it is imperative that ground rules be laid down for media communication reflecting our opinion as to what is in the best interest of the team's performance.
   The team wishes to thank the media for its help and cooperation.

   Frank Garner
   Head Coach

Giving a Good Interview

Saying what you really want to say in front of the camera or microphone in a relaxed and intelligent manner is a skill, which like any other skill, benefits from preparation and practice. In preparing to give interviews, it is a good idea to begin by thinking about the sort of questions that might be asked and to think about how you would feel most comfortable replying to those kinds of questions. We asked each team member to write down a list of possible questions that might be asked at key times: in preparation for the event, before a race, after a race in the finish area, between races, and after the whole competition. We then circulated the questions and requested that athletes mentally review their preferred responses. At the training camp, we set up a role-play situation in which athletes had a chance to act as the reporter and as the athlete being interviewed.

Role playing by team members can be fun. It can give athletes and coaches experience in responding and can also provide good stress-control practice. Videotaping role-playing sessions provides an element of reality, and the tapes can be played back so you can see how you responded and so you can discuss possible areas for improvement. By going through this process, you will enter the real interview situation with some preparation and additional confidence, as opposed to going in "cold."

In the role-play situation you can practice responding to questions in the way you want to respond. You can also practice one-breath relaxation immediately before the interview or, if the pace picks up, during the interview. Knowing what you want to say before you have to say it is one of the most important considerations in giving a good interview, one in which you are relaxed and in control. When you are not certain of what you want to say, you may not leave viewers with a good impression of you or your sport.

Think about what you like most when you watch or listen to an interview. Probably you would like to learn more about the person behind the performance. What is that person like? What kind of human being is he or she? Does he or she think and feel like me? If you can give a little of your human side in an interview, almost everyone's interests are likely to be served.

Some preevent interview questions can be answered in a way that will support your own goals and your own mental preparation plan. For example, when asked the question, "Are you going to win?" what kind of response is going to be most helpful, most constructive, and most comfortable for *you*? Some suggestions that have been offered include: "I've trained well; I'm in the best condition I've ever been in; I'm sure going to try to win"; "My goal is to be in the top 3 (or whatever), and I'll do everything I can to reach that goal''; ''I don't focus on winning, I focus on doing the best I can do under the conditions; the winning takes care of itself''; ''I have worked on a plan to carry me over the distance as fast as possible. I'll focus on that plan and extend fully; that's all anyone can do''; ''The goal of any high-performance athlete is to win the gold, but if we don't, we will be satisfied if we have given our best effort.''

In dealing after an event with questions about losses or setbacks, you can reinforce your general refocusing plan by saying: ''Of course I'm very disappointed. I will have to do a careful evaluation to know what really happened. I will look for the constructive lessons in the loss and then try to set it aside. We have to look forward, not back; we cannot control history.''

If you are feeling a little uptight before an interview, use the one-breath relaxation procedure and focus on what you want to say. If, during an interview, you feel like things are getting a little out of control due to a reporter's cutting you off, giving rapid-fire questions, or becoming rude or hostile, here are a few ways you can deal with it. Take a breath to slow things down. Take a moment to think of a reply, or answer with a question.

If you do not want to deal with a controversial question or issue, you can tell the reporter that you do not want to discuss that issue, or you can suggest that she or he talk with someone else. Standard answers for questions lacking empathy or basic respect for the person being interviewed can also be helpful. For example, in a role-play situation a sports reporter asked Steve Podborski, ''Why did you bomb out last year?'' Steve responded, ''It's a very complicated sport—and that's my standard answer.'' Keep in mind that if you feel the reporter is being unreasonable or disrespectful, most of the listening or viewing audience will feel similarly. Having an acceptable preplanned way to end an interview is also a good idea (e.g., ''I'm sorry, I'm going to have to go now. Our van is getting ready to leave. I enjoyed talking with you. Thank you.'').

Guidelines for Positive Media Contact

George Young, one of Canada's best known sports reporters, expressed his perspective (personal communication) on the sport/media relationship as follows:

- "National team members have a responsibility to cooperate with the media . . . athletes are ambassadors for their sport."
- "The most important thing is to make the media work for you—to promote your sport."
- "Athletes should be prepared to talk to media after a win or after a loss."
- "You can't ignore the media because you've had a poor performance. People at home are interested in you and want to know what happened; otherwise, the media wouldn't bother talking to you."

He also pointed out that reporters tend to seek out—and keep going back to—athletes who speak freely and easily and have something interesting to say. They tend to avoid athletes who don't have anything to say, such as those who give terse yes or no answers or lots of "Uh, well, I don't know, uh you know," offering nothing of concrete interest.

Young offers the following suggestions:

Before the Interview
- To give yourself a little time to think about your answers, ask the reporter what kinds of questions he is going to ask you. (e.g., "What do you want to talk about?")
- Instead of putting reporters down for asking dumb questions, give them a question or piece of information they may not have. Plant a thought, or "feed" the reporter with a few questions such as, "Did you know that this was the best time I've had this year,""Did you know that . . . ?"

During the Interview
- Take your time, especially if you feel pressed.
- Be yourself. Be open, honest, and personable with your responses.
- Talk to the *interviewer*. The camera and microphone will find you.
- If you did have a preinterview conversation with the reporter, avoid saying "Like I said before" during the actual interview.
- Put your answer in words you are comfortable with but that the average viewers/listeners/readers can also understand. Your audience are not experts in your sport, so avoid highly technical terms or jargon.

- Answer with a question if you want to regain control. If a reporter says, "Many people say that . . . ," you can respond, "*Who* told you that?"
- Don't give terse yes or no answers, but also avoid long-winded responses that drag on. Questions should normally be answered in 30 to 50 seconds.

CBC sports reporter Andy Shaw (personal communication) suggests that it might be helpful for athletes to approach media interviews as an opportunity to inform people about their sport and to help them develop an understanding and appreciation of it. He points out that in addition to wanting to learn something about the sport, the viewing audience is looking for details about what happened out there, especially something unusual or interesting that they are not likely to know.

The audience views an event from the outside looking in. They see a race or hear about a result without ever really knowing what it is like to be on the inside. If, within an interview, you can take the audience inside and share some of your thoughts as they occurred during the event, most of the viewing audience will be both informed and satisfied. If you simply describe how the race or event felt from your vantage point, which is something you as athletes can readily do, viewers will have an insight that cannot be gained in any other way.

Athlete's Focus— Four Case Studies

I n this chapter, the action plans for four Olympic athletes are discussed in order to provide you with tangible examples of the value and result of systematic planning and assessment. In each case the content of the initial plan was drawn directly from the athlete's personal history of previous best performances.

These athletes, like others, found that planning in which they drew upon their previous best focus helped both positive feelings and performance outcomes. They also found it necessary to adapt their initial plans and refine their thinking so that they performed well in the variety of situations and challenges that they faced.

As you mature as a competitor, your knowledge of what will work best for you is also likely to mature. Good planning and ongoing self-assessment will speed up the maturation process. It will help you move from thinking and hoping that you will be able to achieve your on-site goals, to knowing and showing that you can do it. Self-knowledge and personal refinement will be an ongoing process.

Case #1—A Winning Focus

I normally tell athletes to focus on what they are doing and on personal goals. The idea is that if you focus on what you have to do, the winning will take care of itself. But there are exceptions in which highly skilled athletes get an additional and helpful ''charge'' by going out to win. That is *not* the central focus they hold *during* the performance, but it is the orientation they take before the event. Case #1 is one such athlete involved in alpine skiing. Her personal goal is ''to win.'' She was skillful enough for this goal to be within reach.

When this athlete was highly charged, determined, and challenged before the event, she had her best results. She seemed to ''perform better in the spotlight . . . I do well because I *have* to . . . I don't have a choice because the challenge is there.'' Her first World Cup win was a good example of this orientation. It indicated what she could do if she got into the right psychological frame. The capacity to perform consistently well was within her grasp if she could replicate this ''charged-up'' prerace feeling and absorbing race focus.

When no one was expecting anything from her, or when she perceived people as having given up on her, she could either accept the challenge or forget it. Under these conditions she had an inclination to forget it—unless she consciously set a personal challenge for herself. For her first World Cup win, she skied after a poor performance by a teammate who was favored to win the race. As she expressed it, ''She blew it. I had to take up the slack, I approached it as if it were my *job*. I was thinking 'It's up to me. I am the only Canadian left with a chance to win.''' Her immediate prerace thoughts were, ''This is it! Do it now or never! Now's your chance.'' She felt that this helped her get psyched to go out and win.

Performance outcomes are always ''up to you'' because you have the capacity to give your best in any event. Wanting to win and going out to win are always up to you. Much of this athlete's prerace psych fell into place as she moved away from hoping to win toward believing that she could win. Once that happened, she made a commitment to go out and turn her beliefs into reality. She seemed to benefit from that kind of ''charge.'' It made her determined to do the job that she was fully capable of doing.

If you are like this athlete, thoughts relating to winning could be tied into your preevent plan in order to generate the kind of intensity that will allow you to win. You may not always come out on top, but at least you will have a good shot at it. If you do not generate the intensity that comes with wanting to win, you can almost be assured that you will not perform to your limit.

So during your warm-up, remind yourself that you want to win, that you are capable of winning, and that you are going to do it. At least you are going to perform at full intensity. You didn't do all that training in order to go out and perform half-charged. The winning focus will raise your activation level and will energize you, both of which should enhance your performance *if* previous best performances have been associated with a winning focus.

You almost always get what you expect. If you expect a bad performance, you are pretty sure to realize your expectation. If your performance expectations are positive or your challenges and goals are set high, you have a much better chance of a high-level performance. This is particularly true for someone like the athlete who had a history of needing to feel "charged up" to perform well.

Prerace Plan

In devising her prerace plan, this athlete had to keep in mind that ideally she wanted to enter races with a high personal challenge and with high expectations. These expectations came from her and from people who were important to her.

Plan A. If her expectations were high or the appropriate challenge was there, or if she was coming from the front or off a good training run, her prerace procedure at the top of the hill shortly before racing was focused the following way. First, to help herself feel activated and "charged up" moments before the start, in addition to vigorous prerace physical activity, she used some of these reminders:

- It's up to me. I can be the best. I want it.
- This is it! Do it now or never!
- Now's your chance!

Next, as she approached the gate, she reminded herself of her desired race focus:

- Me going at the course—not it coming at me.
- Offense, not defense.
- Speed and *not* holding anything back; taking the necessary risks.

As she left the gate, her focus was riveted on *speed—go!*

From that point she focused on:

- *"Looking out"*—seeing the course in segments—everything's connected. Not a lot of conscious thought—no hesitation.
- Focusing *"down the hill"*—"Me in control and going at the hill—not holding back."

Plan B.   If her performance expectations were low as a result of coming from the middle of the pack, or if it was an easy course, or if she was experiencing little doubts or felt that the coach had given up on her, she needed a plan to get things back on track. Some thoughts she used to *switch* into a positive dimension included the following:

- Remind yourself of your track record in *racing*.
- Remind yourself of your potential: "I have skied faster than—or beaten—all of these racers, and I *can* do it today."
- Set a personal goal for yourself that will allow you to ski with no holding back.
- Think of your own capacity and commit yourself to do what you are capable of doing.
- Let that "quiet energy" surface: "I've got a job to do. Do it!"

As you approach the gate, pick up on the prerace reminders from Plan A and follow through with the same race focus plan.

Another strategy she used to help get herself back on track was to watch a videotape of the fastest racers on that hill, that day, while thinking of what she needed to do. Then she could see herself in imagery, "fired up," skiing the way she wanted and needed to ski. This imagery would later be followed by her normal prerace plan. If the training run was not too hot, she reminded herself that the training run is just that—a training run, something to get the kinks out, to check the line, wax, and skis, for example. It is not the race, and when you are a little more "fired up" for the real thing, you can go, even if the training run was poor.

Refining the Initial Plan

Over a period of 2 years, this athlete found that her plan of action worked well in most situations. However, she also discovered that if she was not in a good general frame of mind before the race due to equipment problems, poor performance(s), or communication difficulties with her coach, then thinking that she *had to* do well or thinking about realistically trying to win did not help her performance. Under such circumstances, her attempts to call up winning thoughts or images often resulted in self-doubts. She ended up thinking, "Who are you kidding!" Thoughts like "I *have to* do it," which in other circumstances had helped her to activate, led her to feeling trapped and resulted in less commitment rather than more. She ended up expending much of her energy trying to convince herself that the whole thing was worthwhile rather than believing that she was doing it because she wanted to or liked it and chose to do it.

A prerace focus on "winning" only worked well for her if her equipment, communication, and skiing had been going smoothly. If things had not been going so well, another approach seemed necessary. In a recent World Cup win, even though things had generally not been going well for her up to that point in the season, she skied very well that day. She went into that race without putting any great pressure on herself. In her words she focused on "just having fun, feeling the acceleration and just enjoying it." That day she went faster than any other skier in the world—by a clear margin. While skiing the course, she wasn't trying to talk herself into anything, she wasn't shaky or afraid, and she wasn't making technical errors as she had in the previous couple of races. The "feel" was there when it had not been there in other races.

She learned that she had to draw upon the mental approach most likely to let her perform her best that day. She began to select the relaxed-fun approach when she did not want additional pressure or when she had not been skiing so well and wanted to present a believable image to herself. In this case she focused only on having fun, on accelerating, and on connecting with the hill. She attempted to "just ski and enjoy it and let the results take care of themselves." Using the relaxed approach she was "confident in the start but not overzealous." She was "just ready to go out and do it."

As she expressed it,

I selected the winning focus when I knew [that winning] was realistically within my grasp if I added a little "juice." The focus on winning was the added juice that built on my desire to realize the potential! My prerace thought was wanting to ski fast or enjoy the speed, and therefore win. The word wanting *is too vague. What I mean is that speed can be either endured or relished. I see those terms as defensive and offensive, respectively. When I say that I want to have fun skiing or to enjoy, this isn't being lighthearted or airy, but rather more determined and therefore formidable.*

This athlete discovered that for each approach to work best, it had to be reserved for the right circumstance. She also realized that if one approach did not work for certain situations, she could change it.

Training Focus

This athlete also found that she needed to get "a little more radical during training and not be so concerned with perfection" so that in a race she would be confident about pushing 100%. It was helpful for her to try to fire herself up for some runs in training. In addition to giving her more confidence about pushing in a race, it gave her additional practice at setting a personal challenge and getting herself "up" enough to go after that challenge wholeheartedly. Simulated races in training helped, as did approaching certain training runs as if they were important races where she was willing to be a little less precise, a little more fired up, and really willing to *go*. That is what is required in competitions. You have to train the way you hope to race, which means you must sometimes "race" or at least follow your best race focus in training.

Suggestions for the Athlete

Table 15.1 shows the responses this athlete made to the Competition Reflection form in Appendix A. The responses guided my suggestions. I made two general suggestions to this athlete:

1. Keep the communication going with your coach, even if it is hard at times. For example, make an effort even at those times when you feel that "he isn't even there" during your conversations. (I felt it was important that she catch misinterpretations

Table 15.1   Racing Reflection Responses for the Winning Focus

Case 1

Racing Reflection Responses
1. Think of your all-time best performance(s) and respond to the following questions keeping that race(s) in mind:

   How did you feel just before that race?

No activation (mentally and physically flat)	0 1 2 3 4 5 6 7 (8) 9 10	Highly activated (mentally and physically charged)

Not worried or scared at all	(0) 1 2 3 4 5 6 7 8 9 10	Extremely worried or scared

2. What were you saying to yourself or thinking shortly before the start of that race(s)?

   - *I'm thinking of my first World Cup win.*
   - *This is it! Do it now or never! Now is your chance!*
     The other top ranked Canadian didn't do well—thought it's up to me—only one left. Felt quiet energy.

3. How were you focused during the race (e.g., what were you aware of, or paying attention to, on the way down the course)?

   - *Speed and not holding anything back.*
   - *Taking all the risks.*
   - *Was also thinking these thoughts just before the start. Actual race focus— looking out—course coming at me in segments—everything connected.*

4. Now think of your worst competitive performance(s) and respond to the following questions keeping that race(s) in mind:

   How did you feel just before that race?

No activation (mentally and physically flat)	0 1 2 (3) 4 5 6 7 8 9 10 *Feeling flat led to the worry*	Highly activated (mentally and physically charged)

Not worried or scared at all	0 1 2 3 4 5 6 7 8 (9) 10	Extremely worried or scared

(Cont.)

Table 15.1 Cont.

5. What were you saying to yourself or thinking shortly before the start of that race?

    - *What am I doing here?*
    - *What's wrong with me today?*
      I wish this was over.

6. How were you focused during the race (e.g., what were you aware of, or paying attention to, on the way down the course)?

    - *Struggling against giving up and thinking about how badly I was feeling.*
    - *Most of my energy was focused on getting myself keen and not on what I was doing (skiing). When I had a bad turn, I expected it.*

7. What were the major differences between your thinking (or feelings) *prior* to these races (i.e., best and worst)?

    - *Confidence and lack of confidence.*

8. What was the major difference in your focus of attention *during* these performances (i.e., best and not-so-best)?

    - *Dwelling on the postitive feeling of speed and thinking about the definite lack of it.*

9. How would you prefer to feel just before an important race?

No activation (mentally and physically flat)	0 1 2 3 4 5 6 7 8 ⑨ 10	Highly activated (mentally and physically charged)

Not worried or scared at all	⓪ 1 2 3 4 5 6 7 8 9 10	Extremely worried or scared

10. How would you prefer to focus your attention *during* an important race?

    - *Me going at the course, not it coming at me. Offense not defense.*
    - *Focused down the hill and in control of it. Me being in control and going at the hill.*

(Cont.)

Table 15.1 Cont.

---

11. Is there anything you would like to change about the way you approach a race? or training?

   - *Need to get more radical during training and not so concerned with perfection so that in a race I'm confident about pushing 100%.*
   - *Need to be more fired up—now a little too precise, not willing to really go.*

12. Is there anything you would prefer to change about the way the coach approaches you during training or competitions?

   - *I felt a certain pressure during training runs to be "flawless" and therefore not able to take a chance and perhaps make a big mistake during training. I don't know if this was totally coach-influenced or self—or a combination of both.*

---

before they were blown out of proportion because a lack of good communication with the coach had negatively affected her mood and performance in the past.)

2. Avoid those trapped feelings by reminding yourself that you want to be there competing. You chose to be there. You might as well make the best of it. Have fun skiing. Feel the acceleration. Enjoy. Be the best you are capable of being. (I felt this was important because towards the end of the previous year she was feeling trapped, which sometimes interfered with her determination to really go after a result. However, she *chose* to come back when she could have chosen not to. So she really was doing it because she wanted to, and she was doing it on her own terms.)

Shortly after sending my notes to this athlete, I received the following letter:

I read your notes concerning my approach for this year at a very appropriate time. We had just arrived in the valley and already the coach and I had had a little confrontation, blown out of proportion as it turns out, but I hiked up into the hills and took your notes along to read at a quiet time.

I have to really say, you've managed to make a very concise synopsis of our whole discussion and you're right on base as to my thoughts and the situation. So, thanks for giving me an outline that I can easily refer to if I find myself distracted or unproductive!

By the way, as soon as I got down from the hike I decided to clear up the misunderstanding with the coach, and we both felt much better.

So it's all systems go! I hope I can let the results speak for themselves!!

Case #2—A Relaxed Focus

This alpine skier is probably more representative of the majority of athletes in that she performs best when feeling relaxed and not thinking about the outcome. Her personal racing history indicated that when she had an abundance of unoccupied time before her race, she tended to think about, or worry about, other racers' results or her own performance. This unproductive thinking had resulted in her worst races.

Three of the best performances in her life occurred when her time was occupied right up to race time. Partly because her time was filled, she minimized or eliminated worries about others' expectations of her and where she would place. She was able to leave the start area thinking, "I know the course, I know what I have to do. Just go—do it." It was helpful for her to plan a sequence of activities that constructively filled her time, from the moment she arrived at the hill until the start of her race. In terms of an ideal feeling for the race, she also gained from a long warm-up in which she could be physically active at the top of the hill for several minutes. She was then able to be more ready both physically and mentally at the start.

Race Day Doubts

Because worries or doubts such as "All the name people are here; they are really good," or "Am I good enough?" had sometimes surfaced in the past, this athlete needed a plan for dealing with them. An organized prerace plan minimized these distractions, but some still occurred. One strategy she used for dealing with them was to immediately tell herself, "*Stop, tree it!*," and then focus on something more constructive, such as "I've trained well," "I've prepared well," and "I've developed a detailed prerace and race plan—I'm fully capable of doing it—relax and do it." Her refocusing goal was to get back on track quickly in terms of what she was supposed to be doing at that moment. Usually that meant returning to her prerace plan.

Initially it was helpful for her to remind herself that she couldn't control other racers or other people's expectations. No sense in wasting a lot of energy on that. *But* she could control herself, so it became important to focus on what *she* had to do.

The 20 minutes up the hill in the chair lift had been a time in which worry thoughts began to intrude. We attempted to turn that chair lift into an advantage, or at least no disadvantage. It seemed to me that it was a beautiful time for personal space—the eye of the hurricane. She attempted to view it as a repose, by using that time constructively to relax her body, to focus on relaxed breathing, and to visualize her race. Occasionally, she also chose to use that time for pleasant diversion by focusing on the shapes and forms of the hill, trees, and clouds, by listening to music or singing, or by recalling happy memories.

Race Focus

In her best training runs, she was relaxed and the run unfolded naturally without conscious force. She knew the course, she knew what she had to do, and she did it. Her best focus, going down the hill, was always to look for the next gate. Because this focus had worked in the past, she made plans to recapture it for future races.

When sections of her race had not gone well, her focus had drifted, for example, to seeing the coaching staff on the side or wondering what someone else was thinking or worrying about her placing. If her focus did momentarily drift, she now planned to use that as a signal to get back on track. She attempted to think "gate" and return her focus to the position where it had helped most before (i.e., the next gate). She developed a plan, put it on paper, tried it in a practice situation, then tried it in a race situation. She made the necessary adaptations in the less important races, so she was ready and flowing for the more important events.

First Race Reflections

I was able to meet with this athlete to go over her postrace Competition Evaluation form following the first race of the season. This was her first opportunity to try her race plan in a competitive situation. Having her race evaluation forms in front of us helped considerably.

First Run. I was pleased to see that her first run went so well, especially because it was her first race after a serious injury; plus, her first run (as opposed to the second) had been a problem in competition. Now she knew she could have an excellent first run if she followed her prerace plan and held her preferred race focus.

Her first run was right on target in terms of the plans and feelings she wanted to carry into the event. Let's take a close look at that first run focus. From the moment she started warming up until the finish of the race, her overall thought content was almost 100% positive or self-enhancing in terms of her goal. Going into the race she was, on a scale from 0 to 10, completely determined (9), physically activated (7), and committed to fully extend herself (9). She was feeling mentally calm rather than uptight, and she was in control.

The race focus for the first run worked. She was completely focused or absorbed in the race itself and had an excellent performance result. In her words,

The first run was focused and good. I knew the course well. I did it in imagery on the lift. I knew it so well I could just go for it. I had no time to think of anything—only, get to the finish. I was just thinking about getting to the bottom and everything else was a blur. I wasn't conscious of anything on the side on the way down, just focused ahead. It didn't matter if a turn wasn't perfect, just as long as I got to the bottom fast.

In this race she followed her preferred race focus: "Only on the race, not on how I'll do, or what people will think or say if I perform poorly. Centered on the race and highly activated but free and easy—confident."

Second Run. Unfortunately, her second run proved to be a poor performance. However, in terms of helping us clearly understand what works for her and what does not, to have back-to-back races with such dramatically different performance results was an advantage. It's not something we hoped for but it was something we could take advantage of. Going into this race, she was lacking determination (2), had a low level of prerace physical activation (3), and had no prerace commitment to fully extend herself (1). She was feeling mentally uptight and out of control. Her confidence level was down from the first race, dropping from a 7 before the first race to a 3 before the second race.

Immediately before this run, she was saying "Go for it," but not really believing it. She was saying the same things as for the first run, but did not have the inner confidence that she could do well. She "kind of knew" her second run wasn't going to be as good as the first—before the race—even though she didn't openly admit it to herself.

From the moment she started warming up for this run to the finish of the race, her overall thought content was largely negative or self-defeating in terms of her goal. As she expressed it, she was "distant from the second race—mentally there, but not there—I wasn't up for the run." What influenced the change in her prerace thoughts?

"After the first race the girls were saying it was just the person who got a good wind who did well. So I started thinking, maybe it was just the wind. *Maybe* I can't repeat." This lingering thought, "Maybe I can't," likely set up the loss of preferred race focus that she experienced during the second run.

"The second run was a mental drifter. I thought about what I was skiing like; did I take that turn right? I was trying to make everything precise—thinking about each turn—letting the course come to me—I was conscious of how I was doing, [seeing] people on the side of the course, [thinking] this is a difficult part of the course."

Most of the time during her second run, her focus of attention drifted away from the task in front of her. She was thinking about how she was doing and the way she was skiing. Her attention shifted from just skiing fast, which was the focus she held in the first run race, to evaluating her skiing and herself.

In preparation for her second run, she was questioning her own ability and thinking more about whether the girls were right about the wind than about following her prerace plan. She was "there but not there, mentally"; she was "saying but not believing." The doubts and little voices debating why she did well on the first run interfered with her best race focus. When those doubts surface, it is especially important to fill the time constructively, *making sure* the course is known, using imagery, and warming up vigorously. But she had not followed her planned prerace procedure. Several differences were apparent. For example, when compared with the first run, she used less positive imagery (fewer mental runs) and did not reach the physical intensity she preferred during her immediate prerace physical warm-up.

Lessons Learned

Her prerace plan and race focus plan worked well under a "normal" condition, that is in a situation where others were not saying things to plant doubts in her head. So she kept that plan for normal conditions.

In the doubting situation, she did not get *fully into* her prerace plan or her race focus plan. Her ability did not change from one race to the next, but her confidence in her ability, as well as her prerace physical activation, did change.

To improve her mental set in such conditions, she developed some realistic reminders of her proven abilities. She wrote them down, thought about them in a quiet time, and prepared herself to draw upon them if needed in the competition. Her capacity for using mental imagery was very good, so she also decided to use additional positive imagery of her run or of a previous good run to help serve as a reminder of how she could perform. In imagery she saw herself become all the things she wanted to be for this race, and then, in imagery, she skied that way. She imagined herself being determined, physically activated, in control, relaxed, committed to extend, willing to take necessary risks, and confident in her abilities and in her race plan. If by chance some little doubts did surface before a race, as occurred before her second run, she needed a plan to deal with them. Doubts became a cue to refocus on her prerace preparation plan and to get back to doing what helped her prepare. This allowed her to fill as much of the remaining time as possible with constructive physical and mental activity.

If her refocusing plan had been operating after her initial competition's first run, it would have unfolded something like this: The girls are implying that I skied well *only* because of the wind. Come on now, do you really believe that the *only* reason *anyone* skied well today was because of the wind? Do you really believe that you *do not* have the ability to ski down this hill, **fast**? Who was complaining or planting doubts? Those who had skied slower? Think about what you have done before. Think about your successful runs. Think about your own capacity. You know what you are capable of doing, in any condition. Enough of this! Get back on to your prerace plan. You are going to have a great second run.

Another approach would have been to take the little doubts and "tree them." Set them aside or suspend them until a more appropriate time. They're not even worth wasting energy thinking about now because they won't help you. *Snap back* to your prerace preparation plan as quickly as possible, and you will perform closest to capacity.

When she tied in some confidence-enhancing or happy thoughts before the race and had a plan to deal successfully with the little doubts, she increased her chances of focusing strictly on the course during the race. As a result, she performed consistently closer to her potential.

Refining the Initial Plan

Over a period of 2 years this athlete was very conscientious about developing her mental plans and doing her race evaluations. As a result, she made significant gains in terms of understanding herself and her mental approach to skiing. Toward the end of our first year working together, she sent me the following note:

This season has been very beneficial in that I've learned a lot about myself and the way my mind functions. There have been a lot of good things and of course, a few negative.

I've pretty much figured out my race plan, what helps and what hinders me. For some time I was a little confused as to where I stood. A lot of thought and analysis both personally and also with the coaches has cleared up a lot of vague, unsure areas. The biggest barricade lay in the area of overcoming the bad memories of injury and [fear of] hurting myself again. When I finally accepted that this was a major hindrance, a lot of weight was lifted off my shoulders because I knew that my physical and technical abilities can and will take me to the top. With time, races, confidence, patience, and a little self-pushing, I will soon defeat the negative memories.

Trying to stay very positive and keep self-confidence high is still probably the most difficult, next to the memories mentioned beforehand. Sometimes after a poor race, I find myself wondering what is it all for? The answer

*to that question, I found, was success. One positive result can defeat five
negative ones. I guess the saying "Victory is sweet" is very true!*

*All else seems to be going along quite well. Social relations among all
the team members, including myself, are actually very smooth. A little
"give and take" is all that is required. All in all, I'm feeling quite good.*

I was pleased to hear that her first year had been a good grow-
ing experience in terms of learning about herself and the way her
mind functions through the ups and downs. These are important
life lessons. Really finding out what kind of focus helps or hinders
your performance is a very positive step because that is what allows
you to draw out your physical and technical abilities.

During her second year of mental training, this athlete continued
to gain strength and confidence. She pointed out,

*Before, I was trying to convince myself that I could achieve my goals.
Now I have more inner belief and confidence. Now that I am ranked among
the top skiers, with those who used to be my idols, I feel more confident.*

*Last year I got angry at myself or so upset about not performing well.
Initially if I didn't get angry or punish myself, I would feel guilty, as
if I wasn't taking it seriously. This year I'm keeping it in perspective and
reminding myself what it's for. Now I'm thinking about enjoyment as
well as intensity.*

*This year, for the first time ever, I pushed during a whole training camp.
I never let up. I was always trying to be better than the last time. When
I had a specific thing to work on (e.g., something technical or pushing
in one area of the course), I stayed interested and motivated. When I started
to coast, I stopped, and went free skiing. I don't want to practice skiing
at low intensity.*

At that point everything was on track for this athlete. Mentally
and physically she was strong, organized, and ready. I think she
also gained from recognizing that the important people in her life
would still love her regardless of performance outcomes. This allowed her to settle back, relax, focus, and enjoy it. And that's when
she was freed to perform best. Table 15.2 contains the racing reflections upon which our work was based.

Table 15.2 Racing Reflection Responses for the Relaxed Focus

Case 2

Racing Reflection Responses

1. Think of your all-time best performance(s) and respond to the following questions keeping that race(s) in mind:

   How did you feel just before that race?

No activation (mentally and physically flat)	0 1 2 3 4 5 6 ⑦ 8 9 10	Highly activated (mentally and physically charged)

Not worried or scared at all	0 ① 2 3 4 5 6 7 8 9 10	Extremely worried or scared

2. What were you saying to yourself or thinking shortly before the start of that race(s)?

   - *My time was occupied right up to start of race. I was thinking I know the course; I know what I have to do . . . just do it . . .*
   - *Just ski and flow. I was feeling energized, charged, but relaxed.*

3. How were you focused during the race (e.g., what were you aware of, or paying attention to, on the way down the course)?

   - *Centered on the course only, nothing on how I'd do, or where I stood at that point in the race.*
   - *Always looking for the next gate.*

4. Now think of your worst competitive performance(s) and respond to the following questions keeping that race(s) in mind:

   How did you feel just before that race?

No activation (mentally and physically flat)	0 1 2 3 ④ 5 6 7 8 9 10	Highly activated (mentally and physically charged)

(Cont.)

Table 15.2 Cont.

Not worried   0 1 2 3 4 5 6 7 8 ⑨ 10   Extremely
or scared   worried or
at all   scared

5. What were you saying to yourself or thinking shortly before the start of that race?

   • *I had lots of unoccupied time to think before the race. I worried about other racers, worried about own performance, worried on chair lift up.*
   • *I was thinking you have to do well, just push, don't worry about the others (saying don't worry but always letting my thoughts wander towards other competitors).*

6. How were you focused during the race (e.g., what were you aware of, or paying attention to, on the way down the course)?

   • *I was aware of who was at the side of the course, who was watching me. I was thinking about where I was placing at that point, projecting as to how I would do.*
   • *My focus drifted to coaches on side of course, wondered what they were thinking.*

7. What were the major differences between your thinking (or feelings) *prior* to these races (i.e., best and worst)?

   • *Good:*
     Relaxed, confident, warm, energized, thinking of myself. Just thinking of positive, happy things. Knowing that inside I'm very confident and sure.
     Bad:
     Worried, talking myself into confidence, thinking of how I would do.

8. What was the major difference in your focus of attention *during* these performances (i.e., best and not-so-best)?

   • *Good:*
     Focused—intense, only on the course.
     Bad:
     Thinking about the finish. Worried about not competing well, about what others are doing and thinking.

9. How would you prefer to feel just before an important race?

No activation   0 1 2 3 4 5 6 7 ⑧ 9 10   Highly
(mentally and   activated
physically   (mentally and
flat)   physically
                                                       charged)

(Cont.)

Table 15.2 Cont.

Not worried or scared at all	(0) 1 2 3 4 5 6 7 8 9 10	Extremely worried or scared

10. How would you prefer to focus your attention *during* an important race?

   - *Only on the race, not how I'll do, or what people will think or say if I perform poorly. Centered on the race and highly activated but free and easy—confident.*

11. Is there anything you would like to change about the way you approach a race? or training?

   - *Don't project the finish in a race, think about me only, not others. Have more self-confidence. In training, always pushing limits so it is natural in a race.*

12. Is there anything you would prefer to change about the way the coach approaches you during training or competitions?

   - *Not at this point.*

Case #3—A Consistent Focus

This alpine skier was very inconsistent in her competitive performance because she had a great deal of trouble getting her thoughts focused in one direction. She performed well in training, but as the race approached she had a tendency to become very scattered in her thinking, which affected the consistency of her results. She did not race with the same thoughts and focus that worked so well in training.

To become more consistent in competitions, she first had to become fully aware of what allowed her to perform best—that is, what kinds of feelings and what kind of focus helped most. Second, she had to plan for this focus to occur on a regular basis. Without self-awareness and a plan, her best feelings and focus might happen every now and then, but not consistently enough. Table 15.3 lists her recollections about what focus allowed her to perform her best and what prohibited her from being her best.

Table 15.3 Racing Reflection Responses for the Consistent Focus

---

Case 3

Racing Reflection Responses
1. Think of your all-time best performance(s) and respond to the following questions keeping that race(s) in mind:

    How did you feel just before that race?

    No activation   0 1 2 3 4 5 6 7 ⑧ 9 10   Highly
    (mentally and   activated
    physically   (mentally and
    flat)   physically
                                                                                        charged)

    Not worried   0 1 2 ③ 4 5 6 7 8 9 10   Extremely
    or scared   worried or
    at all   scared

2. What were you saying to yourself or thinking shortly before the start of that race(s)?

    • *Go fast, charge. You're capable of anything! This was one of the few times in my career that I did clear imagery of the whole course (skiing all the way down) before the race.*

3. How were you focused during the race (e.g., what were you aware of, or paying attention to, on the way down the course)?

    • *I was really relaxed, wasn't thinking of anything, except skiing fast. Everything was clear, almost perfect; could see everything coming to me.*

4. Now think of your worst competitive performance(s) and respond to the following questions keeping that race(s) in mind:

    How did you feel just before that race?

    No activation   0 1 2 3 4 5 6 7 8 9 ⑩   Highly
    (mentally and   activated
    physically   (mentally and
    flat)   physically
                                                                                        charged)

    Not worried   0 1 2 3 4 5 6 7 8 9 ⑩   Extremely
    or scared   worried or
    at all   scared

5. What were you saying to yourself or thinking shortly before the start of that race?

(Cont.)

Table 15.3 Cont.

- *Thinking too much about technique, worrying about it. Didn't think about speed.*

6. How were you focused during the race (e.g., what were you aware of, or paying attention to, on the way down the course)?

   - *Sort of frozen, my mind was like an ice cube, wandering anywhere and everywhere at the same time. No consistent focus. I was aware of the coach on the side on the way down. I criticized myself on the way down.*

7. What were the major differences between your thinking (or feelings) *prior* to these races (i.e., best and worst)?

   - *Best:*
     Relaxed *and sure of myself.* Confident *that I could do it.*
     Worst:
     Uptight, mind wandering all over, worried, and too much technique thought.

8. What was the major difference in your focus of attention *during* these performances (i.e., best and not-so-best)?

   - *Best:*
     I knew I was the best and focused on going fast.
     Not so good:
     I wasn't sure I was the best and focused on worry, technique, and self-criticism on the way down.

9. How would you prefer to feel just before an important race?

No activation (mentally and physically flat)	0 1 2 3 4 5 ⑥ 7 8 9 10	Highly activated (mentally and physically charged)

Not worried or scared at all	0 ① 2 3 4 5 6 7 8 9 10	Extremely worried or scared

10. How would you prefer to focus your attention *during* an important race?

    - On just relaxing and skiing fast with a clear mind (no distractions) and confidence in myself!

11. Is there anything you would like to change about the way you approach a race? or training?

(Cont.)

Table 15.3 Cont.

- *My performances are* very *inconsistent from race to race. I would like to be able to always feel the good way, the way I felt for my best races.*

12. Is there anything you would prefer to change about the way the coach approaches you during training or competitions?

- *No, I want to do my own thing.*

General Warm-Up

This skier's better training runs had occurred after a good long warm-up. Her better race performances were almost always on the second run. Even her feeling on her bike improved after she had gone a good many miles. So it made sense to plan a more extensive warm-up before her first race. A longer warm-up, one that got her heart rate up for an extended time, helped her feel more relaxed before the start, and she performed better when feeling more relaxed. Her more extensive general warm-up consisted of cycling or of going for a long easy jog before she got to the hill, then increasing her preevent skiing once she got to the hill.

Prerace Preparation at Top of Hill. Her best races had unfolded when she was physically warm and activated (8) and yet feeling loose, relaxed and *not* worried (3 on the worry scale). Her preference was to be even calmer mentally and less worried (1). Once she started to relax, she skied well. The combination of physical activation and mental calm gave her her best race. For immediate prerace physical activation, she found that starting to get her body *moving* 5 to 10 minutes before the start of her race helped. She wanted her legs and body to feel warm and ready as she approached the gate.

For mental calm she needed some reminders to place and to keep herself in the right thinking space—to have a clear head, relaxed and free from worry. Shortly before leaving the gate, she attempted to draw upon some of the following reminders:

- Ski the way you know you can ski with a clear head, relaxed, in control, fast.

• Take a deep breath—breathe out slowly and think *relax*. You're capable of anything. "You're in control, you're capable, no worries, just go."

The focus she wanted to take down the hill with her was one of trust in her body and in herself. She didn't have to think of anything. She simply had to keep a clear focus on what was coming and let her body go—the way it had been trained to go.

When she freed herself to do that, she had the best run of her life. She "was really relaxed, wasn't thinking of anything, everything was clear . . . almost perfect . . . could see everything coming to me." Her prerace thoughts were to "relax" and "go fast," "you're capable of anything"—which, of course, she was, when she relaxed and enjoyed it. *Technical* reminders at this time did more harm than good.

This athlete was somewhat of a free spirit and didn't want to be overly organized. However, shortly before the race, it was important for her to be sure to prepare herself with the sort of thoughts and feelings that had allowed her to approach her potential in the past. Somehow she had to be sure that these feelings and the resulting clear focus surfaced in race situations. Because of her personality, a cassette tape with music and some focus reminders seemed to be a good option. They would allow her to call upon the basic feeling she wanted without worrying about a moment-to-moment procedure. If you choose to try this option, first use it in training situations so it becomes natural, comfortable, and flowing.

Free-spirited, spontaneous people often prefer to organize less. They don't want to *feel* too regulated or too analytical. This applies not only to free-spirited athletes but also to actresses, actors, dancers, speakers, and singers. These performers will benefit from a specific kind of preperformance state of mind that must be planned for. However, the process they go through to get into their preferred mental state will not likely be highly structured or cognitive in nature.

Dealing With Mistakes.   To ski really well, this athlete said she needed to have "a clear head," a head that was not clouded with other worries. Otherwise it would "show up on my skis." She also mentioned that if she made a mistake, she normally would get very "upset and erratic." On her way to see me one day, she unfortunately put a long scrape in her mom's new car. But she "parked" the car in the lot in front of the gym, and it was completely out of her mind while we talked. She was able to "park" the car and her worries about the scrape (mistake). She no doubt came back to the mistake later on (what am I going to tell my mother?), but she waited until a more appropriate time. She did not let the mistake interfere with our course of action.

When she made a mistake on the hill while skiing, I suggested she attempt to do a similar thing: "park" the mistake, then quickly focus ahead so she could see everything coming to her. She couldn't afford to waste precious time or energy criticizing herself on the way down. She needed her full focus on the course ahead of her because that would allow the very best run of her life. If self-criticism did begin to surface, she could use it as a *signal* to shift attention ahead—to what was coming. What happened on the last gate was no longer within her control, but what happened on the next gate *was* still within it.

I suggested she work on a basic three-step procedure for dealing constructively with mistakes.

1. Park the mistake—put it aside for now.
2. Use it as a signal to shift attention to what is coming.
3. Deal with the mistake after the race by doing a careful postrace evaluation. Learn as much as possible from the mistake so that you have a better chance of preventing that kind of error in the future.

Adapting the Initial Plan

The first year I spoke with this athlete, she thought about developing a prerace tape and a refocusing plan but never actually did it. She continued to ski off the course as she had the year before. But in the process, she learned something about herself and by the next year was more determined to *do* something to improve the situation. She knew she could stay on the course and race fast if she was in the right mental state. She did it at least once that year. Our goal for the next year was more consistent good performance, which was fully within her capacity.

I suggested that she *do* three things:

1. *Make a morning tape.*

   Go through your records and tapes and select the music that is most likely to get you in the right mood or spirit *in the morning*. Select music that will let you feel energized, good, light. Start the race-day morning off on a high note by listening to those songs.

2. *Make a pre-race tape.*

   Make a second tape combining music and reminders that will help put you and keep you in a good mental state for skiing. Use this tape at the top of the hill in the start area before the race begins. In selecting reminders for your tape, think of how you want to feel (e.g., relaxed, calm, clear). If you want to go faster and stay on the course, slow everything down. Slow down inside your head to go faster on the course. Try easier— not harder. Consider the following reminders for your top of the hill tape:

   - It's only you and the hill, relax and enjoy it—nothing else matters.
   - Slow down, try *easy*, it doesn't matter.
   - You're in control, you're capable, relax and just ski—like in training.

3. *Develop a clear refocusing strategy.*

   Outline a strategy for refocusing when you are confronted with worries about speeding up or getting out of control. Use such cues as "tree it," "bench it," or "sit on it" to cue your refocusing on something that works for you. Most important, *practice* using your strategy.

   While this athlete was attempting to implement these mental plans, she discovered that if someone told her to "relax" or if she told herself to relax shortly before the start of the race, it often created more problems than it solved. It made her aware of being excited or uptight and made her feel that her strategy was not working. I suggested that she replace thoughts about relaxation with thoughts about "Butterflies in formation." It's good to feel excited; it's ok to have butterflies. Focus on what you have to do to make them fly in formation. For her that meant reminding herself "to feel and ski like in training," "to focus only on her skiing and to look ahead to the next gate," "to just go like training, put your poles in and power out of the start."

She started this season completing about 40% of her runs and progressed to completing 80% of her runs. She still became "scattered" and went off the course in certain important events, but considering her performance last year, she made good progress. To reach the level of consistency that she and her coach are seeking, another year of conscientious effort aimed at applying her mental plans will likely be needed.

Case #4—A Task Focus

When I first met this athlete, although she had been on two previous Olympic speed skating teams, she had *never* performed as well in an important competition as she did in training or in time trials.

On her Racing Reflections form found on Table 15.4, she outlined the focus that had allowed for her best performances in competition. However, this focus did not result in her performing to the level she had achieved in training. To pursue her potential in competition, she gained by looking closely at her focus method for best performances in training.

In training, which is where she excelled, she just thought about staying low and skating fast. In competitions, this focus often gave way to watching the best skaters and worrying about them, trying to impress the coach, and—sometimes—to thinking in great detail about technique.

After developing and implementing her competition plan, she quickly discovered that her best focus for competition was similar to the one that worked best in training. For example, by reminding herself to "just relax, stay loose, do my best, and that's it," she could carry a perspective that felt good and worked well. Helpful prerace reminders included one or more of the following: "Just be me and skate the best I can," "Focus on me," "Just do what you have prepared to do," "Do my best and that's all." In her initial prerace plan she included a commitment to push to her maximum—"Push your max," "See what you can do when pushing your max," "Go as hard as you can"—and a reminder to focus on her own race and not on other racers. After a number of races she discovered that she did not need a reminder to "push her max." In fact, it tended to interfere with her relaxed flow early in the race, so she deleted it from her prerace plan.

Table 15.4   Racing Reflection Responses for the Task Focus

Case 4

Racing Reflection Responses
1. Think of your all-time best performance(s) and respond to the following questions keeping that race(s) in mind:

How did you feel just before that race?

No activation (mentally and physically flat)	0 1 2 3 4 5 6 ⑦ 8 9 10	Highly activated (mentally and physically charged)

Not worried or scared at all	0 1 2 3 4 5 6 ⑦ 8 9 10	Extremely worried or scared

2. What were you saying to yourself or thinking shortly before the start of that race(s)?

    - *I can have a good race and beat the Russian.*
    - *Just stay low and skate fast.*

3. How were you focused during the race (e.g., what were you aware of, or paying attention to, on the way down the course)?

    - *I was trying to impress my coach.*

4. Now think of your worst competitive performance(s) and respond to the following questions keeping that race(s) in mind:

How did you feel just before that race?

No activation (mentally and physically flat)	0 1 2 3 4 5 6 7 ⑧ 9 10	Highly activated (mentally and physically charged)

Not worried or scared at all	0 1 2 3 4 5 6 ⑦ 8 9 10	Extremely worried or scared

5. What were you saying to yourself or thinking shortly before the start of that race?

(Cont.)

Table 15.4 Cont.

- *I was watching the other skaters, thinking abut how good they were.*
- *I was thinking about impressing my coach.*

6. How were you focused during the race (e.g., what were you aware of, or paying attention to, on the course)?

   - *I was trying to find a way to prevent my legs from hurting.*

7. What were the major differences between your thinking (or feelings) *prior* to these races (i.e., best and worst)?

   - *For the better races I went to the line, thought "just skate" and started.*
   - *In the poorer races I thought too much about how I should be skating technically and about results.*

8. What was the major difference in your focus of attention *during* these performances (i.e., best and not-so-best)?

   - *In the good races I focused only on the positive.*
   - *I said to myself that I was capable, I skate well and I will give my max— that's all.*

9. How would you prefer to feel just before an important race?

   No activation   0 1 2 3 4 5 6 ⑦ 8 9 10   Highly
   (mentally and   activated
   physically   (mentally and
   flat)   physically
                                                          charged)

   Not worried   0 1 2 3 4 5 ⑥ 7 8 9 10   Extremely
   or scared   worried or
   at all   scared

10. How would you prefer to focus your attention *during* an important race?

    - *To not think too much. Just say to myself that I am ready for this race and what will happen will happen.*

11. Is there anything you would like to change about the way you approach a race? or training?

    - Training:
      Yes! To not be afraid to suffer or hurt. In some ways to be a little crazy.
    - In a race:
      Yes! To not let myself be influenced by other skaters and to not be afraid of not having perfect technique at the end of a race.

(Cont.)

Table 15.4 Cont.

---

12. Is there anything you would prefer to change about the way the coach approaches you during training or competitions?

- *Yes! I don't want them to encourage me to work harder by generating hatred towards the countries that beat us. I want to work hard and beat them but not through hating them. They are human, too, like you and me.*

Soon after implementing her new competition plan, she began, for the first time ever, to perform as well in races as she had in training. She actually skated some personal bests in important competitions. After every race, she completed a Race Evaluation form and continued to refine her plans based upon these evaluations. Whenever she felt the need to refine something on her plan, she wrote it on her planning form. The night before her race, she listened to quiet music, relaxed, and read over her revised plan.

She found that her best races occurred when her *only goal* going into the race was to skate well and "stay low." She also felt best within the race when she focused only on "staying low" and "racing her race."

The final thought that she ended up using as she approached the starting line for her best races was, "I have the potion—I have the motion." She generated this phrase herself from the following sheet of jingles entitled "Potions and Motions," which I distributed to members of the national speed skating team at an early training camp. For her, this phrase was all-encompassing. It reflected confidence in her mental plan and her physical ability and reminded her of the focus she needed to carry into the race.

Potions and Motions

Excellence in sport is a mix of potions and motions, psychological potions and physical motions. The biggest problem is that we work on the motions and forget about the potion.

- You need the right potion to have the right motion.
- If you don't have the potion, you won't have the motion.
- Develop a good potion and you will free the motion.

- Draw upon your good potion every time you go through your motions.

Refining the Plan

In her first important international competition after beginning her mental training program, this athlete was able to break the powerful East German domination of women's speed skating. She placed third in a competition where the four East German skaters would normally have swept the first four places.

It is interesting to look closely at what happened to her mental focus during her four races at this competition. In her first three races she followed her basic mental plan very consistently and skated very well each time. Her consistent on-site goal was to "stay low and skate well"; her final thought as she approached the starting line was "I have the potion—I have the motion." And when she was going best in all three races, she was just thinking about "staying low." But in her fourth and final race, her whole pattern changed. She started to think about final outcomes; she worried about other skaters and began to doubt herself. Her goal going into the final race was "to stay in third place." On the strength of her first three races, she did manage to stay in third place. However, she performed far below potential and was over four seconds off the winning time over 1,000 meters, whereas in the previous three races she had been less than .75 seconds off the winning time. She did not follow the race plan that had previously worked so well.

I have outlined on Table 15.5 this athlete's race evaluation responses for her third and fourth races at this competition, both of which were 1,000 meters. I included her comments for both of these races on the same sheet so that an easy comparison could be made.

I met with this athlete after that competition, and together we went over her Race Evaluation forms and discussed what had happened. There were some critical lessons to be drawn out with respect to how thinking affects performance and how important it is to concentrate fully on following an established focus plan that works, especially in situations where much is at stake.

To help her maintain the best race focus in important events, I suggested two things:

1. *Before* a crucial race, remind yourself of what works best. Of course you want to maintain your medal position or to move

Table 15.5   Comparison of Race Evaluation Responses for Two 1,000 Meter Speed Skating Races: Race 3—Good Race; Race 4—Poor Race

1. What was your performance goal for this race?

Race 3   (1,000 meters)—*To skate well*
Race 4   (1,000 meters)—*To stay in 3rd place*

2. To what degree did you achieve your performance goal?

Race 3   0 1 2 3 4 5 6 7 8 ⑨ 10

Race 4   0 1 2 3 4 5 6 7 8 9 ⑩
         Did not achieve   Achieved goal
         goal at all   completely

3. Did you have any other goal(s) for this event?

Race 3   *To stay low*
Race 4   *To skate well, but most thought centered on third place*

4. To what degree did you achieve this other goal(s)?

Race 3   0 1 2 3 4 5 6 7 8 ⑨ 10

Race 4   0 1 2 3 4 5 ⑥ 7 8 9 10
         Did not achieve   Achieved goal
         goal at all   completely

5. Circle your feeling *going into this race.*

Race 3   0 1 2 3 4 5 6 7 8 ⑨ 10

Race 4   0 1 2 3 4 5 ⑥ 7 8 9 10
         No determination   Completely determined
                                            (to achieve goal)

Race 3   0 1 2 3 4 5 6 7 8 ⑨ 10

Race 4   0 1 2 3 4 5 6 7 ⑧ 9 10
         No confidence   Completely confident
                                            (in ability to achieve
                                            goal)

Race 3   0 1 2 3 4 5 6 7 8 ⑨ 10

Race 4   0 1 2 3 4 5 ⑥ 7 8 9 10
         No physical   Highly physically
         activation (flat)   activated (positively
                                            charged)

(Cont.)

Table 15.5 Cont.

6. How did your prerace plan (phase) go?

   Race 3   0 1 2 3 4 5 6 7 8 ⑨ 10

   Race 4   0 1 2 3 4 ⑤ 6 7 8 9 10
             Terrible   Felt really good

   Comments: (e.g., what was on, what was off, what needs work or adjustment?)

   Race 3   *Followed same plan that worked before, worked really well.*

   Race 4   *I thought too much of other racers and about the times they could do. I didn't feel relaxed, started to feel tired and to get a headache. At this point I started to have self-doubts.*

7. What were your thoughts as you approached the start of the race?

   Race 3   *I have the potion. I have the motion.*

   Race 4   *Wake up!*

8. How did your race focus plan (phase) go?

   Race 3   0 1 2 3 4 5 6 7 8 ⑨ 10

   Race 4   0 1 2 3 4 5 ⑥ 7 8 9 10
             Went poorly/   Went really well/
             lack of focus/   completely focused/
             off race plan   followed race plan

9. When you were going best, where was your focus?

   Race 3   *Stay low.*

   Race 4   *Never really went best. During the race I thought about my competitor. I didn't concentrate.*

10. Were you able to fully extend yourself during the race (how much did you push)?

   Race 3   0 1 2 3 4 5 6 7 8 ⑨ 10

   Race 4   0 1 2 3 4 5 ⑥ 7 8 9 10
             Did not extend   Completely extend
             myself at all   myself (to the limit)

up to a higher placing, but what will allow you to do that? Remind yourself to follow your race plan, "race your race," "stay low."

2. If your thoughts do drift to worries about other highly skilled athletes or to your placing, have a refocusing plan that will allow you to stop these thoughts and replace them with a more constructive focus. For example, say to yourself, "Stop—that won't help," and then shift your focus to the specific things that you know help you to skate well. Remind yourself of the approach that has already worked for you."Race your race." "You have the potion—you have the motion."

Refocusing Plan

The speed skater used the refocusing plan below to regain her appropriate competition focus. These strategies successfully redirected her attention from distractors to more valuable cues.

Worry About Competitors Before the Race.

- They are human just like me. We'll see what they can do in the race, not in warm-ups or in training. I need to focus on my *own* preparation.
- All I can do is my best. Nobody can take that away from me. If my performance is good, I'll be happy. If it's not so good and I tried, I shouldn't be disappointed.
- I'm racing for *me*. It's *my* max that I want.

Worry About Competitors During the Race.

- If I start to think about others during the race, I'll shift my concentration to *my* race, *my* technique: "stay low—race your race."
- "I have the potion—I have the motion."

Preevent Hassles.

- Skate blades don't cut the ice—carry a small sharpening stone to pass over the blades.
- Delay in start—if I'm already on the ice and it's likely to be a short delay, jog around, keep moving, stay warm, do a mini-warm-up with some accelerations. Follow my normal prerace plan when approaching the line.
- Windy or snowy conditions—it's the same for everyone. Just go out and do what you can do.

Worries During Competition.

- Poor start—no problem, it can happen. It's not the start that determines the final result. Follow your race plan. Push your max.
- Not hearing a split time—it's ok. Just skate well and race your race.
- Pain in the legs—shift focus to the specifics of the task being done: the steps in the turn, pushing the blade to the side, pushing hard to the finish line.

We also looked at her race plan and considered where she might be able to pick up the .5 to .7 second that separated her from the top. She decided to introduce a "pick-up" point at the 200- and 600-meter marks to maintain her pace; she also felt that she might benefit from a refocusing strategy for the last 100 meters, to ensure that she finished the race having nothing left. I suggested that for the last 100 she come up with a cue that could be tied into her race plan and that in training she practice focusing on power and pushing herself for the last 100 meters of simulated races, while maintaining good technique. Her revised Race Focus Plan is outlined in Table 15.6.

I felt that this athlete made very good progress on her overall focusing skills in a very short period of time. With additional work on refocusing, she was able to stay on track even in situations where everything in the competition seemed to rest on her final-event performance. If she can stay physically healthy, her mental strength is likely to carry her to her goals.

Table 15.6 Race Focus Plan to Implement a "Pick-Up" Point in Speed Skating

	First 5th Start → Transition	Second 5th	Third 5th	Fourth 5th	Final 5th Kick Point Final Push for Finish
Prestart					
Think:	Push hard (blade to side)	Stay low "*pick up*" to maintain "PACE"	Stay low "*pick up*" to maintain speed	Continue to push hard	"*Let's Go!*"
"Relax."	Fast steps		Push (blade to side—controlled power)	Stay low	Push max (blade to side)
"Skate well."	Stay low, gain speed, relax		Stay relaxed	Maintain pace	Pick up rhythm
"Stay low, especially on the corners."					"*Give Everything*" (push the 10) just to the other side of the line
"I have the potion. I have the motion."					Stay in control but really give everything that's left

Life
After Sport

When you no longer look forward to or enjoy being involved in sport at a high-performance level, it is time to move on to another phase of life. As one of our top former Olympic athletes said while reflecting upon his competitive years, ''You have to enjoy what you are doing. As long as you enjoy it, you cannot look back and say, 'I wish I had never done it.'''

What will you do with your life after you stop competing in sport? If you are uncertain, or worried about this eventuality, you are not alone. Almost all high-performance athletes approach retirement from sport with some uncertainty, fear, or sense of loss.

Sometimes these feelings follow the attainment or loss of long-sought goals and dreams. But do not despair. There is life after sport. You can lead a happy and productive life outside of sport if you know what to expect and plan the necessary adjustments.

Post-Olympic Slide

Whether or not you achieve your performance goal, you are likely to experience a flat time or down time after a major event like the Olympics. The down time simply comes sooner after a loss than after a victory. You've been working for many years for an ultimate or bigger-than-life goal, and suddenly it is finished. On the way to the goal, your time has been incredibly organized and filled.

Your wake-up times, eating times, training times, sleeping times, meeting times, and competing times have all been regimented. A high percentage of your life has been scheduled around a single purpose, a purpose that is now gone—temporarily for some, permanently for others.

After the hoopla of parties, closing ceremonies, congratulatory gatherings, media, and other attention, it is highly likely that you will encounter a time of adjustment, a temporary down time, a gazing-into-space time. After you have been riding a high or living (or living for) a dream, the normal chores of daily life outside the dream may at first feel mundane and not very meaningful. The reasons for that are numerous. The intensity of the event and preparation for it can leave one mentally and physically fatigued—drained. The removal of an important goal can leave one feeling temporarily without direction. With loss, there may be an initial sense of feeling, ''All that work for nothing, for a dream never realized.'' With victory, there may be a sense of wondering, ''Is that all there is?'' or a sadness in knowing the dream has come to an end. For those who retire, regardless of outcome, there is likely to be a dramatic change in the daily schedule in which you have centered around a specific, all-encompassing goal. That in itself is a major adjustment.

Immediately after the Los Angeles Olympics, I went down to the beach in Ventura, California. It was a beautiful, sunny day and the surf was huge. I became totally immersed in those waves. I thought to myself, ''This is a great way to recover from the intensity of the Olympics in which you can experience the full range of human emotion in any one day. You rejoice with those who achieve their goal and silently suffer with those who do not.''

For me, the beach was great post-Olympic therapy because it was physically demanding. I had to swim hard to get out through the breakers and, later, to get back to shore; it required my full focus. If I did not watch the waves closely and adapt to their demands, they would crash into me or over me with incredible force. Once past the point where the waves break, I could float in a most gentle and relaxed free-flowing state.

As I floated, I thought that many of our athletes could have gained from this surf therapy, particularly those who had not fully realized their dreams earlier in the day. But, I had been told that for administrative reasons, they were being bused to the Olympic village right after lunch. It was a good decision for administrators, a poor decision for athletes' heads, I thought. While floating and being caressed by the ocean, a group of our athletes appeared on the beach, much to my delight, defying the law of the schedule and following the law of their hearts. For a couple of glorious hours they were refocused, refreshed, rechallenged, rejuvenated, and fatigued by the surf and sun and by an occasional cold beer. Now they were in a better mental state to go back to the village and to face what lay beyond.

Adapting to the Change—Short-Term

- Expect a period of adaptation after a major event; it is normal.
- Allow time for rest and recuperation—a few days or weeks seemingly "wasted" or dreamt away.
- Stay physically active, but reduce training intensity—do long slow jogs, go cycling.
- To ease the adjustment, try to do something that will hold your attention and fill time in an interesting or enjoyable way—a week-long canoe or camping trip.
- It will help if loved ones also anticipate your natural down time, help arrange for initial positive diversion or a more lasting alternative focus, and provide overall emotional support.

Retirement

Penny Werthner, a good friend, mother, former graduate student, and former Olympian, did her thesis on the retirement experiences of 28 of Canada's best athletes (1985). All had ranked among the top six in the world, many had been medalists in world championships, and some were world record holders. Half were men and half were women; all of them retired from international competition between 1976 and 1982. These former Olympians were asked to rate, on a 10-point scale (10 being perfect), three periods in their lives: while competing, immediately after retirement, and now (at the time the interview was conducted). The average rating for "while competing" was 7.6, that for "immediately following retirement" was 4.4, and that for "now" was 8.0.

A down period, a period of readjustment after retirement, is likely to occur. But there is life after sport, a life that for most athletes equals or rises above the overall life satisfaction experienced as an international athlete. Even those athletes in this group who really "bottomed out" at 0 upon retirement came back up within a couple of years. It's important to keep that in mind as you approach retirement and especially during the down times you may experience in the first stages of readjustment to another focus.

One athlete expressed the situation he faced as follows: "You go from being one of the top players in the country on one of the top teams in the world . . . You go from being extremely competent in something to now being just like the rest of the world, you've lost the edge." Another said that upon retirement she was "a little depressed. I was nobody all over again and I had been a somebody. That was a little sad, but I was doing something really different that demanded most of my concentration, so I really didn't have a whole lot of time to get upset."

An athlete who went through "a really bad depression" said, "A lot of it had to do with my sense of control over my life. My self-esteem wasn't there. So much of my identity was wrapped up in being an athlete. Now it was me, nobody, who didn't know what she wanted, who had no control over her life whatsoever." With "no concrete skills," trying to find a job was very frustrating for her. People would say, "It's nice that you've done well in sport (been an Olympian), but what skills can you offer us?"

She went from a life rating of 8.5 while competing to a life rating of 2 upon retirement. She did, however, come back up to an 8.5 in both life satisfaction and self-confidence within 3 years. How did she move from a very low 2 to an 8.5? "Through a lot of hard work, and a lot of thinking. Part of it, for me, was gaining recognition in something other than sport, feeling competent. Now I feel I have quite a bit of control over what's happening in my life—more so than when I was training." Her experience is an important reminder for other retiring athletes. No matter how down you are—and this athlete hit rock bottom—there is hope that you can work through to new successes.

Another athlete indicated that her first shock was the lack of routine, and that, second, her fitness level dropped; she didn't do anything for quite a while. She didn't hit a depression until she started thinking that she "wasn't anybody anymore," but she "eventually realized that I'm still the same person, even if I don't do really well.'' As soon as she realized that she was still a valuable person, ''finding out that you could be happy within yourself'' and running were enough to lift her spirits and make her happy again. Finally, through pregnancy and childbirth, she felt she was ''totally released from everything.'' Coming to the realization that you have real value and worth as a human being *quite apart from your sport performance* is probably the most critical step in making a healthy adjustment.

Adapting to the Change—Long-Term

Part of the problem in moving out of sport is the uncertainty about stepping out of something at which you are extremely good into something unknown or something in which you have not yet proven yourself. This uncertainty probably lowers your overall confidence upon retirement and contributes to worries about the future. You no longer have a specific goal, and you no longer have a set routine. Most athletes felt that ''having something to go to, to do, another goal, was a very big help.'' ''You might feel a loss, but it is less devastating if you can redirect your energies.'' ''Set another goal, identify another task, and get on with it.'' One athlete said her life went from a 3 immediately after retirement to a 9 within 2 years. When asked how she moved from the 3 to the 9, she responded, ''I applied myself with the same degree of energy as when I was in sport—I worked hard at the university and at my job. I worked hard at my relationship.''

A former world champion and world record holder said that in order to make the adjustment smoothly and quickly, ''I knew I had to redirect my energies very quickly or else I'd start to be depressed. I felt a loss, but it's like going from high school on to something else, I know I'll never be back there again, and it would be foolish to keep going on at it. I was a little bit let down for a while. I had to take a breath before I went on to the next phase of my life. I don't have pangs wishing I could be in there; I know I can't be and have to accept that and carry on with something else. I knew that was it—I'm not going to make any comebacks.''

He seemed to be able ''to put it away'' by redirecting his energies toward something else. That made the loss manageable and the transition relatively quick. He never had any real problem with the transition. "Weeks after retiring I wanted to go forward, just as in competition—the same philosophy. Having a coaching job helped." About a year after his retirement he said, "I feel quite good about things, about the way things are going for me career-wise. There's a lot out there."

A former Olympic gold medalist who never went through a difficult time adjusting said that she knew other athletes had had problems and didn't want it to happen to her. "I wanted to get right into something else. I had a new direction right away, was excited about going to school and trying a new sport; it was a new challenge for me."

A big part of the solution is simply giving yourself a chance to get fully involved in something else. It is not that you *can't* do it, it's just that you have not had the *opportunity* to do it. Once you recognize this and begin to apply yourself in other areas, feelings of competence and personal meaning begin to resurface. The reality seems to be that if you can apply some of your sport dedication to almost any other endeavor, you will have an excellent chance of succeeding. Most people don't work that hard at anything.

Personal Control

An interesting finding in Werthner's (1985) study was that most athletes' ratings of their personal control *rose* immediately following the end of their sports career, and *continued to rise* for several years thereafter. This initial rise was largely due to the lack of perceived control they experienced as competing athletes. The following remarks express typical feelings: "I had very little self-control when on the national team. I was following guidelines. When I stopped competing, the control was in my court." "The coaches had total control of my life while competing; they [told me] when to train, when to eat. I have much more control over my life now." "I was just carried along by the system—it wasn't until the end of my sport career that I took a little bit of control." "I take direction of my own life now, rather than looking to people to give me direction."

A restricted amount of personal control and personal choice while competing accounts for part of the problem in transition. If others do virtually everything except train and compete for you and make all major decisions for you, you do not get much practice at directing your own life. Yet you will need self-direction skills upon retirement and for the remainder of your life. No one will tell you what to do or when or how. No one will make your schedules, arrange your trips, meals, training times, or anything else. You will be responsible for yourself; you'll do it, or it won't get done.

The potential for increased personal control is something most athletes can look forward to upon retirement. It can be a wonderful gift. It can also pose an initial problem, particularly if you did not have much practice at self-direction during your competitive years, because you may not be sure how to direct that personal choice. As soon as you begin learning to direct personal choice toward your own fulfillment, your life will begin to come together, and your life satisfaction begin to rise.

Other things being equal, an athlete who experiences a higher degree of personal control and self-directed choice while actively competing will usually have a smoother adjustment with less "down" time. The more you direct your own life and choices while competing, the more likely you will know how to direct your life choices upon retirement. That doesn't mean that the transition will be easy, but it means that one major obstacle—your lack of experience with personal control—will be removed. Consequently, the adaptation will likely be smoother and faster.

Making the Adjustment

You, along with coaches and loved ones, can help yourself with the transition process by remembering the following:

1. A sense of loss or uncertainty is normal to experience upon retirement from sport. As athletes express it, "It's human nature to feel that way. You can get over it but you cannot get around it." "There is no magic solution; you have to go through those stages; some people just go through them faster than others." "Be a realist. Realize that there are steps to be taken, instead of saying 'I can achieve that perfect adjustment right now.'"
2. A new or absorbing involvement that you feel is meaningful or that can hold your focus will help immensely with the transition. Athletes mentioned such things as going to school,

retraining for a new career, working, physical and recreational activities, or becoming pregnant and starting a family as contributing to a renewed sense of meaning. Something new or absorbing that involves you in a focused way can serve different purposes. It can take your mind off the losses associated with sport retirement; it can give you a renewed sense of personal control or purpose; it can lift confidence; and it can contribute to your overall life satisfaction.

3. A direct attempt to apply to another endeavor some of the lessons gained from pursuing sports excellence will help. For example, make use of the strategies you acquired while competing. Approach new goals with determination, persistence, a positive outlook, and constructive self-talk. Apply some of the strategies for stress control and for refocusing that you developed through sport.

4. Support from important people whose caring extends beyond your performance such as boyfriends, girlfriends, family members, and supportive coaches, can help with the transition process. It can be a great help simply having someone with whom to talk who will listen and lend support.

5. A higher sense of personal control and choice *while competing* will help. Having some say in directing your own life and goals during your competitive years will give you a head start in the years thereafter.

The greatest personal gains mentioned from being an international athlete included a sense of discipline and dedication, self-confidence, increased self-awareness, and self-respect. These are gains that certainly have the potential to be carried for life and that can be transferred into other activities. Think of them as *transferable* rather than static, and they will likely help.

One of the advantages of retirement is that you will have the opportunity to do a number of things that you were unable to fully enjoy as a high-performance athlete. You will have more choice and more options—more time for family, loved ones, career development, school, recreational activities, and community involvement. When you travel, you will get to see the country and enjoy the people, rather than being locked into the training center or competition site. Things that might have been losses while competing can become gains in your life after sport.

The Last Act (or the End and the Beginning)

W hat are you going to do now that you have finished reading this book? My hope is that the end of this book is the beginning of meaningful action that will carry you closer to your goals.

Start by focusing your efforts on anything that jumped out at you, where you said, "That's me" or "That would help me." Plan to refine those areas first. Refinements in those and other areas will help you get the best out of yourself and the most out of your life, but only if you choose to *act* upon them.

It takes an incredible commitment to become a high-performance athlete. There's nothing wrong with saying, I don't want to do all that mental and physical training. But there is something wrong with thinking you can get to the top without doing it. You will never be able to reach the top without developing your mental strength. If you can't make the commitment to push your limits mentally and physically, then adjust your goals, avoid the frustration of consistently falling short of your dreams, and enjoy sport in a more recreational level. That, too, is a worthy pursuit.

If you are really prepared to commit yourself to your goals in sport and have already begun to plan and act on some of the suggestions presented, my experience tells me you will make significant strides towards attaining those goals. I encourage you to remember the basics:

- Go after your own dreams.
- Set specific goals.
- Plan your path.
- Imagine success.
- Act as if you can.
- Mentally prepare for training.
- Train to compete well.
- Focus on what makes you go best.
- Assess your progress.
- Learn from your experiences.
- Refine your plans.
- Be persistent.
- Express your feelings.
- Accept yourself.
- Enjoy your experiences.
- Prepare for your life after sport.

To all of you from all of me—
Smile; you are on the right path.
My best for your best.

Terry Orlick

Planning Sheets

Goals

---

1. Dream Goal (long-term)—What is your long-term dream goal? What is potentially possible in the long term if you stretch all your limits?

2. Dream Goal (this year)—What is your dream goal for this year? What is potentially possible if all your limits are stretched this year?

3. Realistic Performance Goal (this year)—What do you feel is a realistic performance goal that you can achieve this year (based on your present skill level, your potential for improvement, and your current motivation)?

4a. Goal of Self-Acceptance—can you make a commitment to accept yourself and to learn from the experience, regardless of whether you achieve your ultimate performance goal this year?

4b. If you do not meet your desired performance goal, to what extent will you still be able to accept yourself as a worthy human being?

    Complete self-   0 1 2 3 4 5 6 7 8 9 10   Complete and full
    rejection   self-acceptance

5. Can you set an on-site goal of best *effort* (giving everything you have that day) and be satisfied with achieving that single goal?

6. Focused Psychological Goal (this year)—What do you feel is an important goal for you to focus on this year in terms of your psychological preparation or mental control? Some examples are a *specific* goal related to psychological readiness for the event, focus control within the event, distraction control, confidence, coping with hassles or setbacks, and improving interpersonal harmony or relationships.

7. Daily Goal—(A) Set a personal goal for *tomorrow's* training session. Write down one thing you would like to do, accomplish, or approach with a special focus or intensity. (B) Can you set a personal goal before going to *each* training session this year?

8. What do you think you or others could do to increase the harmony among team members this year?

Competition Reflections

These questions are designed to help you reflect upon your personal competitive history and to help you develop or refine a precompetition plan and a competition focus plan.

Knowing your competition self

1. Think of your all-time best performance(s) and respond to the following questions keeping that event(s) in mind:

    How did you feel just before that event?

    | No activation (mentally and physically flat) | 0 1 2 3 4 5 6 7 8 9 10 | Highly activated (mentally and physically charged) |

    | Not worried or scared at all | 0 1 2 3 4 5 6 7 8 9 10 | Extremely worried or scared |

2. What were you saying to yourself or thinking shortly before the start of the event(s)?

3. How were you focused during the event (i.e., what were you aware of or paying attention to while actively engaged in the performance)?

4. Now think of your worst competitive performance(s) and respond to the following questions keeping that event in mind:

    How did you feel just before that event?

    | No activation (mentally and physically flat) | 0 1 2 3 4 5 6 7 8 9 10 | Highly activated (mentally and physically charged) |

    | Not worried or scared at all | 0 1 2 3 4 5 6 7 8 9 10 | Extremely worried or scared |

(Cont.)

Competition Reflections (Cont.)

---

5. What were you saying to yourself or thinking shortly before the start of that event?

6. How were you focused during the event (i.e., what were you aware of or paying attention to while actively engaged in the performance)?

7. What were the major differences between your thinking (or feelings) prior to these two performances (i.e., best and worst)?

8. What were the major differences in your focus of attention during these performances (i.e., best and not-so-best)?

9. How would you prefer to feel just before an important performance?

   No activation   0 1 2 3 4 5 6 7 8 9 10   Highly activated
   (mentally and   (mentally and
   physically flat)   physically charged)

10. How would you prefer to focus your attention *during* an important performance?

11. Is there anything you would like to change about the way you approach a competition? or training?

12. Is there anything you would prefer to change about the way the coach approaches you during training or competitions?

Personal Precompetition Plan—Content

Decide what kinds of activities, thoughts, or images you will include in each category below. Draw upon what has worked for your best past performance and upon what you think will be most helpful or most appropriate for the upcoming competition(s).

General physical warm-up	General psychological warm-up	Preevent physical preparation	Preevent psychological preparation

Personal Precompetition Plan—Sequence

Outline your on-site preevent plan as you would like it to occur at the competition site. List activities, self-suggestions, etc., in the order you intend to do them. Draw upon the material you developed for your personal Precompetition Plan—Content Sheet.

General warm-up—physical and mental	"Start" preparation—physical and mental

Event Focus Plan—Content

General Guide: Decide how *you* want to feel and focus during the event. Then devise a focus plan to allow that to happen. Draw upon what has worked for your best past performances and upon what you feel will work best for the upcoming competition.

Start	First few moves	Remainder of routine program, match, bout, course, event	Last few moves (finish)

Race Focus Plan—Content

General Guide: Decide how you want your race to unfold. Then devise a focus plan to make that happen. Draw upon what has worked for your best past performances and upon what you feel will be most helpful for the upcoming race.

First 5th

Final 5th

Start	Transition	Second 5th	Third 5th	Fourth 5th	Kick point	Final push for finish

Game Focus Plan—Content

General Guide: List the critical situations you are likely to face within the game. Then indicate how you would prefer to respond to each of these situations (e.g., what would be your ideal on-court response?) Draw upon what worked best for previous best performances in that situation. Think of a focus or cue word that will allow you to focus properly to bring on your preferred response.

Critical situation	Preferred response (on court, field, ice)	Focus or cue word to bring on preferred response

Event Focus Plan—On-Course Format
(Alpine Skiing)

Start Area	First few gates	Course	Last few gates finish

FINISH

Race Focus Plan—On-Course Format
(Paddling)

Outline your race plan as you would like it to occur. Include your cues and focus points at various stages in the race.

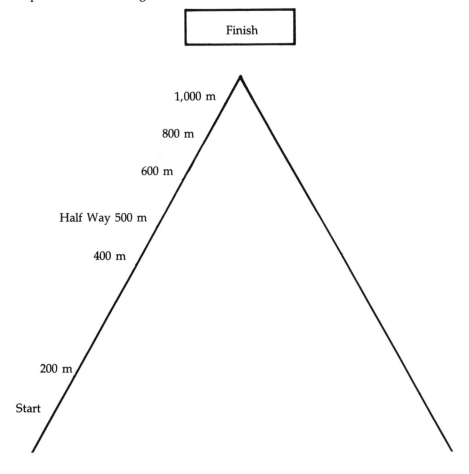

Refocusing Plan

Preevent hassle

Non-ideal conditions

Delay in start

Poor start

Loss of ideal focus in event

Mistake in event

Poor performance (first run, routine, period, event, half, inning)

Poor overall performance (in the event or game)

Other areas

Competition Evaluation Form A

Name: _____   Event: _____

Date: _____   Results: _____

Site: _____   Your Placing: _____

Complete this form as soon as possible or feasible after the completion of each event.

1. How did you feel about your performance in this event?

2. Did you have a performance outcome goal (or result goal) for this event? If so, what was it?

To what extent did you achieve this outcome goal?

Did not achieve   0 1 2 3 4 5 6 7 8 9 10   Achieved goal
goal at all   completely

3. What was your on-site focus goal for this event (e.g., what was the focus you wanted to carry into this event, the one that you felt would likely give your best result)?

To what degree did you achieve this on-site focus goal?

Did not achieve   0 1 2 3 4 5 6 7 8 9 10   Achieved goal
goal at all   completely

(Cont.)

Competition Evaluation Form A (Cont.)

4. Circle your feelings going into this event.

Goal Determination

No determin-
ation   0 1 2 3 4 5 6 7 8 9 10   Completely
                                                          determined to
                                                          achieve goal

Activation

No physical
activation (flat)   0 1 2 3 4 5 6 7 8 9 10   Highly phys-
                                                          ically
                                                          activated
                                                          (charged)

Worry

No worries or
fears   0 1 2 3 4 5 6 7 8 9 10   Extremely
                                                          worried,
                                                          scared, or
                                                          afraid

Control

Completely out
of control   0 1 2 3 4 5 6 7 8 9 10   In complete
                                                          control

Uptight

Mentally calm   0 1 2 3 4 5 6 7 8 9 10   Mentally
                                                          uptight

Focused On Task

No task focus   0 1 2 3 4 5 6 7 8 9 10   Complete
                                                          task focus

Commitment To Push (Limit)

No commit-
ment to fully   0 1 2 3 4 5 6 7 8 9 10   Complete
extend myself   commitment
                                                          to fully ex-
                                                          tend myself

Confidence in Physical
Preparation

No confidence
in my physical   0 1 2 3 4 5 6 7 8 9 10   Complete
preparation   confidence in
(doubts   my physical
                                                          preparation

(Cont.)

Competition Evaluation Form A (Cont.)

Confidence in Psych
Preparation

| No confidence in my mental preparation | 0 1 2 3 4 5 6 7 8 9 10 | Complete confidence in my mental preparation |

Confidence in Abilities

| No confidence in my abilities (to achieve goal) | 0 1 2 3 4 5 6 7 8 9 10 | Complete confidence in my abilities (to achieve goal) |

Risk Taking

| Not willing to take necessary risks | 0 1 2 3 4 5 6 7 8 9 10 | Willing to take neces- sary risks |

5. Did you follow a previously practiced *precompetition plan* (e.g., specific preevent warm-up, positive self-talk)?

_____ Yes _____ No, not at all _____ partly

If partly, which parts were followed and which not followed?

6. What were you saying to yourself (or thinking) *immediately before* the start of the event?

7. Were you able to follow your preplanned *competition focus plan?*

_____Yes _____ No, not at all _____partly

If partly, which parts were followed and not followed?

8. Rate your overall feeling of effectiveness at the competition site and during the different segments of your preevent preparation and perfor-

_____

(Cont.)

Competition Evaluation Form A (Cont.)

mance. Use a scale from 0 to 10 where 10 is "going great" (right on target), 0 is the "absolute pits" (right off target) and 5 is somewhere in between.

30-60 min. before event (general warm-up)	Warm-up before start	Moments before you start
Rating _____	Rating _____	Rating _____
Start	Event	Finish
Rating _____	Rating _____	Rating _____

9. Were you able to fully extend yourself to the limit during the event? (Did you draw from the well?)

Extend limits

Did not extend
myself at all   0 1 2 3 4 5 6 7 8 9 10   Completely
extended my-
self (to the
limit)

10. What were you saying to yourself or focused on to extend to the limits? (or to try to extend limits?)

11. During the event did your focus of attention stay on your performance (following event focus plan) or drift to other things?

Event focus

Drifting most
of the time   0 1 2 3 4 5 6 7 8 9 10   Completely
focused, ab-
sorbed in per-
formance
(following
event plan)

12. When you were going best, where was your focus?

13. If you were going less well in parts, where was your focus?

(Cont.)

Competition Evaluation Form A (Cont.)

14. Did you have to make a recovery to get back "on track" during the event? (or before the competition?) If so, were you able to recover and focus again quickly? If you used a "cue word" to refocus, did it work?

15. Did *anything* unforeseen or unexpected happen (or anyone say anything to you) either before or during the event that may have had an impact on your performance (for better or for worse)?

16. Should anything be changed or adapted for the next competition?

Competition Evaluation—Form B

Name: _____   Event: _____

Date: _____   Results: _____

Event/Site: _____   Your Placing: _____

1. Did you have a performance outcome goal for this event?

2. If so, to what degree did you achieve this performance outcome goal?

Did not achieve   0 1 2 3 4 5 6 7 8 9 10   Achieved goal
goal at all   completely

3. What was your on-site goal(s) for this event (e.g., what focus did you want to carry into this event)?

4. To what degree did you achieve this on-site focus goal(s)?

Did not achieve   0 1 2 3 4 5 6 7 8 9 10   Achieved goal
goal at all   completely

5. Circle your feeling *going into this competition.*

No determi-   0 1 2 3 4 5 6 7 8 9 10   Completely
nation   determined

No confidence   0 1 2 3 4 5 6 7 8 9 10   Completely
                                                                              confident

No worries   0 1 2 3 4 5 6 7 8 9 10   Very worried

No physical   0 1 2 3 4 5 6 7 8 9 10   Highly phys-
activation (flat)   ically activat-
                                                                              ed (positively
                                                                              charged)

6. How did your precompetition plan go?

Terrible   0 1 2 3 4 5 6 7 8 9 10   Felt really
                                                                              good

Were you feeling the way you wanted to feel?

(Cont.)

Competition Evaluation Form B (Cont.)

7. What were your thoughts as you approached the start of the event?

8. How did your competition plan focus go?

Went poorly/lack of focus/off plan	0 1 2 3 4 5 6 7 8 9 10	Went really well/com- pletely focused/ followed plan

Comments (e.g., What was on, what was off, what needs work or adjustment?)

9. When you were going best, where was your focus?

10. Were you able to fully extend yourself during the event (how much did you push)?

Did not extend myself at all	0 1 2 3 4 5 6 7 8 9 10	Completely extended my- self (to the limit)

11. Did you have occasion to draw upon a *refocusing plan* at any time for this competition (before, during, or after)?

Yes _____   No _____

If Yes, comment briefly (e.g., were you able to call upon plan, did it work?)

(Cont.)

Competition Evaluation Form B (Cont.)

12. Did you experience any communication or interpersonal problems surrounding this event

Yes _____   No_____

If so comment briefly (i.e., What was the problem and were you able to deal with it adequately?).

Mental Imagery Questions

---

1. In preparing for your all-time best performance, how much mental imagery did you do?

    None   0 1 2 3 4 5 6 7 8 9 10   An extensive
    amount

    Much less   0 1 2 3 4 5 6 7 8 9 10   Much more
    than normal   than normal

2. About how many times did you "see" or "feel" yourself running through your event (or parts of it) in imagery?

3. When you use mental imagery, what do you see or feel? Do you "see" an image, "feel" a sensation, or both "see" and "feel"?

4. If you use imagery to "see" yourself run through your performance skills, do you see yourself from the outside (as if watching a video) or from the inside (as if you are actually inside yourself performing)?

    Inside view   0 1 2 3 4 5 6 7 8 9 10   Video view
    Half-and-half

5. How clear are your images?

    Very   0 1 2 3 4 5 6 7 8 9 10   Crystal
    unclear   clear

6. How strong are the feelings or sensations associated with your imagery?

    No   0 1 2 3 4 5 6 7 8 9 10   Strong
    feeling   feelings

(Cont.)

Cont.

---

7. When you try to imagine yourself doing something or feeling something, is it easy or difficult for you to control the ''feeling'' or picture?

    Very   0 1 2 3 4 5 6 7 8 9 10   Very
    difficult   easy

8. *Comments?*

Note: It is interesting to note that before all-time best performances, alpine skiers have tended to use more mental imagery than normal (whatever normal may be for that person).

Precompetition Tapes and Self-Suggestions

T he following preevent tape scripts were designed for athletes to use on-site shortly before the beginning of the competition. They could also be used several hours, days, or even weeks before the competition. Some of the suggestions listed could also be spoken by the coach to the athlete sometime before the event.

Our preevent tapes usually consist of a combination of music and self-suggestions, although in some cases they include only one of those elements. Highly individualized suggestions and well-chosen music can give an athlete an advantage if they allow her or him the best chance of entering the competition in a personalized ideal mental state for performing.

Consider starting your tape with some relaxing music, followed by reminders of your good training, past best, and personal potential. Follow that with more energizing music, music you find very enjoyable, and end the tape with a final positive thought(s), such as you are ready, you are your best (or the best), you can do this, go after it, do it!

Suggestions should be recorded in your own language, in your own voice or the voice of another person in whom you have considerable faith (e.g., a personal coach).

If you have a tendency to become too worried before important competitions, *do not* select music or self-suggestions that are likely to raise your anxiety level. Use calmer, more peaceful music and more reassuring thoughts. If you need a shot to pump up or energize, select faster music, and in your suggestions emphasize challenge, your ability to meet the challenge or the importance of the outcome. Individualize it.

Athletes who use tapes generally listen to some of their favorite music in their hotel room before leaving for the competition or on the bus while getting to the competition site. Upon arrival, they do their general warm-up and then listen to their preevent tape. In the case of paddlers, they then put away their cassette, pick up their boat, and go out on the water for their final preplanned, pre-race warm-up. As they approach the starting blocks for their race, they generally repeat their final personalized prestart cues to themselves. These cues are the ones that they have found to be associated with their previous bests.

It is important to test your tape under simulated competition conditions to see that their timing, length, and feeling are right. Make use of time trials for testing and refining your tapes.

Preevent Tape—Sample 1 (for reinforcing belief in self)

1. *Relaxing Music* or relaxation script to hold attention and have calming effect.
2. *Set of Self-Suggestions* to reassure and to focus.
   - You have *every reason* to believe in yourself, as a competitor and as a person.
   - You are well prepared. You are physically ready. You are mentally ready. You have the capacity to achieve your goal.
   - You are fully prepared to extend yourself to meet this challenge.
   - Focus on what *you* have to do and on what *you* are going to do.
   - Focus on what is within your control.
3. *More Music*—energizing music to hold focus and raise activation to desired level, or more relaxing music to lower activation level.
4. *Final Suggestions* (before moving to final on-site warm-up).
   - You are better than you have ever been. You are *stronger,*

you are *more powerful*, you are more mentally ready. Nothing will stop you, nothing will get in your way. You will perform as you have chosen to perform.

Preevent Tape—Sample 2 (for reinforcing belief in collective effort)

1. *Relaxing music* or relaxation script to hold attention and have calming effect.
2. *Set of Self-Suggestions* to reassure and focus.
   • Because of our commitment and complete preparation for this event *we* are ready for a superior performance—physically and mentally.
   • We have developed a highly refined competition plan to take us to our goal.
   • The challenge before us will require a supreme effort. We are fully prepared to give *all* that we have—to push to our limits.
   • My teammate(s) is (are) in superb physical condition and is (are) highly motivated to achieve our goal, just as I am. Together we will do it. Together we are one.
   • Alone each of us is strong. Together we are stronger. We bring out the best in each other.
3. *More Music*—energizing music to hold focus and raise activation.
4. *Final Suggestions* (before start of competition).
   • Trust your teammate(s). Trust yourself. Together you have every reason to feel confident. Nothing will interfere with our perfect harmony (and synchrony). Nothing will prevent us from following our game plan, extending our limits, and reaching our goal. We will do it together, together we are ''won.''

Additional Self-Suggestions to Consider

Stated in First Person (I)

• The challenge before me will require an all-out effort. I am fully prepared for the challenge; I will push my limits.

- Because of the physical preparation I have done *and* the mental plan I have developed, I have an advantage.
- I *can* draw upon all my resources.
- I *will be* as I choose to *be*.
- I *choose to be my best*.
- I *choose to be the best*.
- As I prepare to start, I will become completely concentrated and absorbed by the task. I will feel energized and in control. I will follow my plan. Nothing will disturb me or distract me.
- During training for this event, I prepared my body and mind for a superior performance.
- I planned and prepared my precompetition warm-up to create an ideal feeling state for my performance.
- I developed a refined competition plan to take me to my goal.
- I simulated my performance physically, mentally, and tactically. So I am ready.
- I have every reason to feel confident. I am good. I am better than anyone here. I am the best. I am fully prepared. I am confident in my preparation, and I am completely determined to achieve my goal. People are expecting me to do well, and I am going to show them what I can do.

Stated in Second Person (You)

- Stand tall! Let the champion within you push forward.
- You are already starting to feel the way you want to feel, and you will perform the way you want to perform.
- You are and will remain mentally calm, alert, and absolutely determined throughout.
- You have a well-practiced plan that will unfold as you have imagined, hoped, and planned.
- If you experience any anxiety before the start, it will be transformed into the explosive power of your start.
- You are capable of adapting and refocusing in the face of any obstacle.
- You can control what you do.
- In the competition you will follow your plan, and you will be focused and in control throughout.
- You can control your own destiny.

Self-Suggestions to Enhance Confidence

Some of the self-suggestions listed for the precompetition tapes could also be used by athletes who lack full confidence in their ability. If this is your case, choose, adapt, or develop a list of self-statements that you would like to fully believe (you are strong, you are powerful, you will be as you choose to be). Put them on a tape, repeating each statement several times in a row. Listen to the tape when in a completely relaxed, receptive state. That often occurs after a deep relaxation session before going to sleep.

When developing or choosing personalized suggestions to solidify confidence, think of why you have a right to feel confident going into the event, and remind yourself of that. For a specific self-hypnosis procedure to follow, including a script for attaining a relaxed, receptive state, see the chapter on Self-Hypnosis in *In Pursuit of Excellence* (Orlick, 1980).

Recorded self-suggestions can also be used to prepare mentally for training sessions. Consider the following reminders:

- You are determined to get the most out of each training session, both physically and psychologically, because that will take you to your goal. You want to go to the competition knowing that you have done the work. You *want* to train with the highest quality of effort and look forward to showing the results of your quality training in competition.
- To achieve your ultimate goal, you will have to *extend* yourself in training, you will have to *stretch* your limits. But your goal is realistic and you *can* achieve it.
- You will commit yourself to achieving your training goals. You will focus on specific areas of improvement, extend yourself in training, and perform as you have never performed before.
- In training and in competition, you will feel the way you prefer to feel and perform the way you prefer to perform. You are in control.

Lost Preevent Tapes

What happens if you prepare a preevent tape and then can't find it when you need it at the competition site? Treat it as you would a piece of your equipment, and you will not likely lose it. But in case of loss or breakdown, perhaps it would be worthwhile to carry a copy of your tape or a written copy of your preevent self-suggestions as a backup. If you end up not having a copy of your tape to listen to or a copy of your self-suggestion to read to yourself, go to your memory. Sit down quietly in your own space and think about how you want to feel. Try to recall your major self-suggestions. That should not pose a problem, because as a result of your previous experience with the tape, your self-suggestions should be well learned by this time.

R E F E R E N C E S

Cleary, M. (1984, March 14). Reporters take chances on Torvill and Dean. *The Ottawa Citizen*, p. 37.

Crookenton, I. (1982, December). *Errors in tennis*. Paper presented at the National Sports Coaches Conference, Hamilton, New Zealand.

Griffiths, A. (1983, April). Athletes and reporters depend on each other. *Champion Magazine*, 1, 7-8. Canadian Olympic Association.

Mahoney, M.J., & Avener, M. (1977). Psychology of the elite athlete: An exploratory study. *Cognitive Therapy and Research*, 1(2), 135-141.

Orlick, T. (1980). *In pursuit of excellence*. Champaign, IL: Human Kinetics.

Rotella, J.H., Gansneder, B., Ojala, D., and Billing, J. (1980). Cognitions and coping strategies of elite skiers: An exploratory study of young developing athletes. *Journal of Sport Psychology*, 2, 350-354.

Werthner, P. (1985). *Retirement experiences of elite Canadian athletes*. Unpublished master's thesis, Department of Kinanthropology, University of Ottawa.